MAXIMIZING BUSINESS GROWTH

Your Fast Track System for Achieving Exponential Business Growth in Any Economy

Russ Holder

Maximizing Business Growth: Your Fast Track System for Achieving Exponential Business Growth in Any Economy

ISBN: 978-1-939315-01-4
ISBN-10: 1939315018
ISBN-13: 978-1-939315-01-4

DEDICATION

I would never be so ungrateful to list only my name on the cover of this work, for without the help of so many people over the past 15 years, this book would not be possible.

There are countless teachers, mentors, clients, and friends whom have both inspired and taught me so much over the years... thank you all.

The dedication of the book will go to my family: my mother, Donna Hodge; my late father, Charles Wayne Holder; my step-father, Donald Hodge; and to undoubtedly the sweetest woman who has ever lived, my grandmother, Irene Crowson.

SPECIAL THANKS

I would also like to express a special thanks to several of my friends for helping me put together this project: Shana Sapp, Denise Chiasson, Brenda Schiro, and Duane Pierce.

CONTENTS

Chapter 1:

Your Business Reality Check

The US Small Business Administration shares with us some unfortunate news about business failure:

- 31-40% of businesses fail within two years.
- 49% won't make it to the five year mark.
- Between 65-80% never see their 10th anniversary.

Even if your business stays afloat, there's no guarantee that you'll make money. According to BizStats, 95% of businesses fail to exceed $1,000,000 in annual revenue.

To drive home this reality check, there was a 17.2% increase in small and mid-size business failures in 2007, and that number grew even more in 2008 to 19.7%. Finally, business bankruptcies were up 19.4% in 2007, climbing another 65% higher in 2008.

The last few years has proven that it's not just small and medium size businesses that are failing. Over the last few years some of the largest and seemingly most successful businesses have failed, filed bankruptcy, or have had to merge with other businesses. Even worse, some collapsed because of market conditions or mismanagement.

Here is a brief list of major business failures of the last few years:

2007: American Freedom Mortgage, Bombay Company, CompUSA, NetBank, New Century Financial, Sentinel Management Group.

2008: Circuit City, Countrywide Financial, IndyMac Bank, Lehman Brothers, Lenox, Linens 'n Things, Mervyns, Sharper Image, Tropicana Resort and Casino, Wachovia Bank, Washington Mutual.

2009: BearingPoint, Charter Communications, KB Toys, Nortel Networks, Silicon Graphics, Stanford Financial Group, Trump Entertainment Resorts.

Take a look at a list of the Fortune 500 companies of 1980. It's almost unimaginable that 54% of those companies are no longer in business today. The point is that there are no guarantees that a business will be around forever, no matter who they are or how successful they have been, or even how successful they appear to be today.

But let's not focus completely on failure. Let's shift our attention to the odds of being successful in business.

In his book *"Jump Start Your Business Brain"*, author Doug Hall compares the odds of business success with different forms of gambling:

Gambling Activity:	Chance of Winning:
Slot Machines	32%
Business (six year average)	37%
Horse Racing	41%
Blackjack	45%
Roulette	47%
Blackjack (card counting)	50%

That's unbelievable, isn't it? With the exception of playing the slots, the odds of succeeding in business are lower than coming out ahead when gambling at the casino or track.

The purpose of this book is to help you beat those odds. Armed with the tools you'll discover here, you can dramatically increase your chance of success while building a business capable of incredible growth in sales, profits, and market share.

WHY BUSINESSES FAIL

As a business owner, entrepreneur, or manager, it's natural at this point to ask a very direct and important question: Why are all these businesses failing? That is a great question, but there seems to be some argument among certain experts as to the most common reasons for business failure.

Over the last few years you may have heard business experts, executives and politicians say that businesses are failing because they lack capital; that they don't have the money they need to continue operating. Not to be sarcastic, but don't you think you can keep almost any business running indefinitely as long as you have money to throw into it?

Another common and generic reason often cited for business failure is poor management practices. Again, this is a very broad category, and without specifics it doesn't tell us very much.

In my interactions with entrepreneurs and business executives, there are several complaints I hear most often about our current business environment. Read through this list of problems with your business in mind. How many of these issues are prominent in your business?

PROBLEM 1: INCREASED COMPETITION

It's true, we live in the most competitive time in the history of commerce. If you turn back the clock and compare today's marketplace with that of 25 years ago, there is an average of 50-80% more competition in just about every industry or profession.

There are over 500,000 business start-ups in the US each year. The internet has made it easier than ever to start a business, and if you include all the single operator, home-based businesses that start every year, the total number of new businesses will likely double to over 1 million.

What about your marketplace? Chances are that the competition is tougher than ever before, and this factor certainly impacts the number of business failures each year.

PROBLEM 2: DECREASED CUSTOMER LOYALTY

Along with the rise of competition in the marketplace, another trend plaguing business owners is the decreasing amount of loyalty among buyers. There many factors effecting the perception of customer loyalty. I use the word "perception" simply because measuring loyalty is not a science.

For most business leaders, loyalty is important in how it translates into additional sales and referrals. A loyal customer is great, but a customer that purchases repeatedly from your business is what you really want. For that reason I focus on the metrics of repeat purchases and customer purchase frequency.

Newer technologies such as the internet have changed the way many products and services are discovered and purchased. And in this information age, factors such as convenience and speedy service have become increasingly important to both consumer and business-to-business customers.

Think about a couple of important points that research has uncovered:

- Each year there are over 26,000 new products and brands introduced in the US.
- 74% of so-called "loyal" customers buy outside of their favorite brands.
- 16-30% of consumers change brand loyalty in just one evening of watching commercials.

Instead of thinking about customer loyalty, focus on repeat purchases. With this shift in thinking it becomes much easier to measure and plan your marketing efforts and their success.

PROBLEM 3: ECONOMIC RECESSION

At the time of this writing, the slow economy is causing many businesses, both large and small, great pain and concern. Increased fuel and commodity prices are driving costs up and profits down. Research conducted by USA Today pointed out:

- There was a 17.2% increase in business failures in 2007, and a 19.7% increase in 2008.

- 54% of businesses report slowing sales and customer traffic.
- 79% report business is getting worse.
- 42% are experiencing cash flow problems.

How has the economic recession affected your business?

PROBLEM 4: ADVERTISING AND MARKETING FAILURES

A common complaint among business owners and executives is that their advertising and marketing activities are no longer producing the same results. Many report that response rates have been cut in half, or even more. This is due to several key factors:

- The market is desensitized to most advertising and marketing because they suffer from advertising overload. Buyers are exposed to 2,000-3,000 marketing messages daily, so we've learned to tune them out. I've heard this described as "advertising radar", and I think it is a fitting and accurate description.
- Penetration of almost every major advertising medium is declining as buyers have more television and radio options than ever. Not only that, technologies such as Digital Video Recorders and satellite radio have made it possible for consumers to avoid commercials altogether.
- Almost all advertising and marketing within a specific industry looks and sounds just like every other ad in that industry. I call this "me-too" marketing, and will expound on this later in greater detail.

What about your ads and marketing activities? Are they easily distinguishable from all the other "clutter" in the marketplace? Are they even reaching your target market?

PROBLEM 5: INCREASING MARKETING AND CUSTOMER ACQUISITION COSTS

Compared to 20 years ago, the cost of attracting and acquiring customers has tripled. If it cost you $100 dollars to get in front of a prospective customer then, today it cost $300. Now take into account that marketing effectiveness has fallen dramatically. Twenty years ago it took four attempts to get in front of a buyer, today it takes 8.4 attempts.

It now costs three times more money to get just half the results!

It is getting more difficult to reach your target market, there is more competition today than at any other time in the history of commerce, and it's not going to get any easier.

US Bank, in cooperation with the Small Business Administration, surveyed several hundred failed small business owners, essentially asking "Why had they failed?" Here is the top reason they gave: Lack of vision and the strategy to implement that vision.

They lacked a system for marketing and sales. Notice they didn't say "no marketing and sales." They said they didn't have a systematic approach to marketing and sales. They lacked an effective system to monetize their clients.

The reasons for business failure are very important. By understanding how others have failed, we can prevent the same misfortunes from happening to us.

Maybe you've heard of Michael Gerber and his book "*The E-Myth: Why Most Small Businesses Don't Work and What to Do About It.*" It is the all-time bestselling book on small business and entrepreneurship, and if you haven't read it already, get a copy and start reading it (as soon as you finish this book!).

To paraphrase Gerber, he states that "Most entrepreneurs and small business owners fail because they spend too much time working in their business, and not enough time working on their business." They spend most of their time bogged down in day-to-day operations, putting out fires, and basically operating in reactive mode. They need to be putting more effort into the things that will grow the business, like marketing and sales. This is sage advice from the man widely considered to be the world's foremost expert on small business.

To accelerate and deepen your understanding, I want to simplify business failures as much as possible...

A business needs only two things to be successful: customers and cash. Think about it: How many business problems can't be solved by increasing profitable sales?

There are two primary reasons businesses are unsuccessful. The first is that they lack effective customer acquisition and retention systems. They don't attract enough qualified prospects to their business, and they fail to convert those prospects into profitable, repeat customers.

The second primary reason businesses fail is because they lack effective business management practices. The owners or managers of the business don't operate as effectively, efficiently, or as profitably as they could. When you break it down, almost all business failure can be attributed to these two reasons.

A BUSINESS DEVELOPMENT SOLUTION

There is a reason why I chose the title "*Maximizing Business Growth*" for this book. There were several other title options I considered that were more clever or cool, but none touch on the purpose this book serves more than this simple and direct title.

Maximizing business growth is what this book is about. Through this book you will learn how to gain control over the growth of your business and get the greatest return on investment for your marketing dollar. You will discover how to create a comprehensive marketing plan focusing on specific key areas of your business that will give you the greatest long-term growth in sales, profits and market share. You will learn how to apply the laws of compounding to your marketing efforts to create incredible synergy. You will discover that building and growing a business is much easier than you ever thought possible.

I've been told that I see marketing differently than most people. I've been told this by Fortune 500 executives, Inc. 500 entrepreneurs, advertising and marketing agency bigwigs, and even other marketing professionals and consultants. Frankly, I take this as a compliment.

You can find a hundred definitions of marketing, and while many are good, I like to keep things simple. I see marketing as the comprehensive process of creating lifetime customers.

Yes, there are many sub-processes in such a broad description, but that's what makes the TriFecta Exponential Growth Model so powerful. When you gain control of the Nine Growth Keys in this model, not only is business development simplified, but growth is guaranteed.

When you systematically apply the business development and marketing principles found in this book, you will see results in the nine key areas (Nine Growth Keys) that have the most impact in the growth and success of your business. These successes build upon each other to drive even more success.

This book is divided into three sections. In the first section you'll learn the basics of the TriFecta Exponential Growth Model. You'll learn how the Nine Growth Keys fit precisely into the model and activates the laws of compounding and synergy to maximize the results of your marketing efforts.

The second section of the book will dig deeper into each of the growth keys, explaining how they work both individually and collectively, as part of the model. You will get ideas how to apply these growth keys to your business, and multiple examples of how they have been applied successfully with my clients.

The final section of this book shows you how to put everything you've learned into a nice, neat package. This package is your comprehensive marketing plan, and it will direct your marketing efforts while providing you with measureable and sustainable growth.

The value of this book doesn't end there. This system can be your companion to a lifetime of business success.

DISTINGUISHING YOURSELF FROM A LITTER OF COPYCATS

One of the primary reasons businesses fail at marketing is because they practice the most common form of marketing, which I call "Me-Too" marketing. Many marketing decision makers don't understand some of the key concepts that drive marketing results, so they look for examples from within their own industry. Basically, they do exactly what everyone else in their industry is doing.

Pick up the yellow pages, any business directory, industry publication, etc. Browse through it, find any business category that has several pages of listings, and then try to distinguish one business from another. They are often so similar that if you removed the name, address and phone number of the business from the ads, even employees of the companies wouldn't be able to tell them apart. It is a recipe for failure to copy the terrible marketing of other businesses in your industry. After reading this book you should never again make the mistake of appearing just like everyone else.

DEFENSE AGAINST A HOSTILE ECONOMY

Competing in today's volatile marketplace is becoming progressively more difficult... and that's without a recession to worry about.

Marketing is the driving force of your business, and during a recession, effective marketing is the difference between business failure and incredible success. Your best growth opportunities may very well present themselves in the middle of a recession. In fact, recessive economic conditions have spearheaded hyper-growth for many companies in almost every industry. You just need to know how to use the recession to your advantage. This book will show you how.

Difficult economic times provide a wonderful opportunity to learn new and innovative marketing strategies, and how to maximize your marketing budget and efforts. Take advantage of this opportunity. Commit yourself to becoming the smartest marketer in your marketplace and you will learn that good marketing will compensate for many other business mistakes.

THE TRIFECTA EXPONENTIAL GROWTH MODEL

In *Maximizing Business Growth*, you will learn a new and comprehensive approach to business development called the TriFecta Exponential Growth Model. When put into action, this model will help you achieve rapid, sustainable growth while building a business immune to economic fluctuations. You will increase your top and bottom line no matter what the economy is doing, and you'll have total control of the process.

When you follow the TriFecta Exponential Growth Model, you are proactively driving the growth of your business. You won't find yourself in the unfortunate and weak position of having to react to market conditions and competitors. You will be in the driver's seat making intelligent and informed decisions in the best interest of your company and employees.

Compared to a business that operates in a reactive mode, a proactive, innovative company is in a much stronger position.

You may have to completely re-think your current marketing strategy, but don't let that intimidate you. You are about to learn a system that takes the guesswork out of marketing, and once a few key strategic initiatives have been completed, marketing will become easier than ever before.

As you read this book, think about how each strategy and marketing activity may apply to your business. Let go of your ego and embrace your creativity while you customize these powerful tactics to fit your business. Keep a notepad handy as you read so you can take notes and create your own "To-Do List." If you read this book proactively, not only will you gain dozens of ideas for growing your business, you're going to have a lot of fun, too.

MOVING FORWARD

What can you expect from this book? Results. How can I say this? Because I've seen the results... many times. On half a dozen occasions I've seen growth rates of 300% or more achieved from established companies in less than a year.

Realistically, your business probably doesn't have the infrastructure to handle that kind of hyper-growth. That's OK.

The TriFecta Exponential Growth Model can be managed, tweaked, and turned off and on as needed. As you will discover, achieving annual growth rates of 30-50% is very easy for most businesses with this system.

Most things in life that are of value don't come without effort, so I won't promise you this will be easy. I think "simple" is a more appropriate word. This information isn't rocket science, but if it were "easy", then everyone would be doing it.

If I told you that growing your business were easy, it would imply that you won't have to do anything to achieve results, and it doesn't work that way. However, if you apply the principles of the TriFecta Exponential Growth Model to your marketing efforts, significant growth will come easier than ever before.

The principles that make up the TriFecta Exponential Growth Model aren't difficult to understand or implement. Mastery of anything requires time and effort, and you will never be perfect at marketing. You don't have to be. This system focuses on making small, realistic, consistent improvements over time that culminates into spectacular growth. With the TriFecta Exponential Growth Model, good is good enough.

You can do this. If you've ever developed any skill, you can achieve business success using this model. All that is required is an understanding of simple concepts, reading instructions, following examples, and putting it into action in your business.

WHO CAN BENEFIT FROM THE TRIFECTA EXPONENTIAL GROWTH MODEL?

Often when speaking with groups of business owners, executives and entrepreneurs, I tell them that they *will* definitely understand everything that I share with them. The content of the

TriFecta Exponential Growth Model is completely logical. They *will* understand it, and they *will* agree with me. These principles *will* work for their business if they put them into action.

Will your business benefit from the TriFecta Exponential Growth Model? Actually, I don't know... but here's a quick way to find out. Ask yourself a few questions:

- When all of your competitors have one or two methods of generating new prospects and customers, would you like to have a dozen that all work well?
- Do you want to be able to quickly respond to all the different conditions in today's volatile marketplace?
- Do you want to take the guesswork out of all your marketing decisions, practically insuring you never make another bad marketing decision?
- Do you want to lower stress rates associated with the growth and success of your business?
- Do you want to increase your company's growth rate?

Think about other areas of your life where you've had success. Maybe you're an athlete or a musician; maybe you were an excellent student. It doesn't matter what it is, but any area of achievement in life requires you to learn basic skills first, then expand on them. And that's how it is with marketing a business.

In almost every company I've ever worked with, just about everyone is working very hard, from the CEO to the support staff. But if you don't have the tools you need to master each area of your business, you are working harder, not smarter. If you have the desire to succeed and work hard, this book will give you the tools you need to work smarter. It will give you complete "how-to" instructions to create massive and exponential growth. You just need to provide a little effort to make it happen.

This system is based on universal business principles, so it will work for just about anyone who has the ingenuity to apply it. Many of the examples I give will be easily adapted into your business, while others will require some creativity.

Everybody thinks their business is different. When applied to the context of the TriFecta Exponential Growth Model, very few businesses really are different. I've only found a couple of businesses that could not put this model and system to work for them, and with a little creativity, you will get it, too.

When you do put the TriFecta Exponential Growth Model to work for your business, you will launch yourself miles ahead of just about everyone in every industry or profession. Very few of your competitors, if any at all, understand how to effective apply the law of compounding to grow a business, the dynamics of a comprehensive marketing program, and how to manage exponential growth. These principles and concepts, when applied properly, can literally double a business in a very short time.

As a consultant I have never evaluated a business under $100M in annual revenues that put all of the Nine Growth Keys into place. In fact, only a handful implemented half of them. Don't make the mistake of believing the TriFecta Exponential Growth Model is obvious to everyone. **Of the hundreds of business and marketing executives that I've worked with, I can count on one hand how many had marketing programs designed to create exponential growth. That's too bad, because they were not getting even half the results their efforts could produce.**

After reading this book you will have the knowledge and tools to be one of the elite few who know how to maximize your business growth and dominate your marketplace. That's what you want, isn't it?

Chapter 2:

The Mindset for Maximizing Business Growth

The world we live in is changing faster than ever before, and our business environment is no different. Advances in technology have changed the way business is conducted in many industries, competition is more brutal than ever, and buyers are more sophisticated and educated. To be successful in today's dynamic marketplace, it is vital that you continually change, improve, update and tweak your sales and marketing skills.

Maximizing Business Growth was written to make marketing and growing your business easier and more efficient. The principles and techniques within these pages have been tested and proven in hundreds of businesses, many just like yours.

This book will not make you a marketing expert, but it will provide you with tools you can use to significantly increase your sales, profits and market share. Armed with this book and the

TriFecta Exponential Growth Model, you will reduce the time, effort, and money that it takes to achieve your business goals.

In this chapter I will introduce you to the 10 Maxims for Maximizing Business Growth. These are skills, qualities and concepts that the most successful business leaders possess. If you are able to adapt these qualities, it will make growing your business a much easier endeavor.

Some of these maxims will be very familiar to you; others may not. A couple of them are so important that I devote separate chapters to understanding them. The better you commit yourself to following these 10 business proverbs, the easier it will be to create the business of your dreams.

MAXIM 1: IT'S ALL ABOUT RESULTS

As the title implies, this book is about maximizing the growth of your business. It's about producing real, measureable and quantifiable results of increased sales, profits and market share. There is nothing in this book that is a distraction from achieving these results.

To achieve your full growth potential you need to adopt the same focus on results. Most people are process or task focused. Exceptional entrepreneurs and business leaders are focused on achieving results and goals.

One of the reasons entrepreneurs fail to get the results they could is due to poor planning. You see, successful entrepreneurs are people that make things happen. They take action and they drive forward. Many times their approach to sales and marketing is "Ready? Fire! Aim."

I don't want to hassle entrepreneurs too much for this, because in general this isn't a bad trait. However, it's important you understand something: to maximize the growth of your business and get the most profitable results for your efforts, you are going to need to plan. When you're striving to produce the greatest results in the shortest amount of time and for the least amount of financial investment, you need to have coordinated efforts. This will not happen by accident.

You have to plan to Maximize Business Growth. Success doesn't happen by accident.

I would like to make you a promise. I promise you will grow your business easier and more efficiently than ever before if you do just three things:

1. Take the time to read this entire book.
2. Create a business development program based on the TriFecta Exponential Growth Model.
3. Take action to build a comprehensive marketing program.

You will be using the same process I use when consulting with clients and you will become more effective, efficient, and successful in whatever business you are in. You will get results.

MAXIM 2: WORK SMARTER, NOT HARDER

Often times when I'm speaking to groups I will ask my audience, "Who in this group would like to double their profits in the next year?" Of course almost everyone raises their hand. Then I tell them, "Keep your hand raised if you are willing to double the number of hours you are working now." Of course, almost all hands go down.

As an entrepreneur, business leader or manager, it's likely you're already working 40+ hours per week. To grow your business you can't just work harder, you will have to work smarter.

This book will help you work smarter. Doesn't it seem smarter to structure your marketing so the same efforts pull twice the results? I'm going to show you how you can use the TriFecta Exponential Growth Model and the Nine Growth Keys to create incredible marketing synergy. You will put the Law of Compounding to work for your business, making it possible to achieve exponential growth.

If you're an executive, entrepreneur, sales or marketing manager, or if you run a professional practice, this book will make your life easier. If you play any role in marketing, selling, or running a company or department, this book will provide you with direction and strategies essential for growing and strengthening your business or department.

Have you ever heard of the book, *"The E-Myth: Why Small Businesses Don't Work and What to Do About It."* Written by Michael Gerber, it is the all-time bestselling book on small business, and I recommend it to all business owners, executives, and aspiring entrepreneurs.

Although Gerber makes many insightful points in this book, one of them is very pertinent to the concept of working smarter, not harder, and that point is this:

"Most entrepreneurs fail because they spend too much time working IN their business, and not enough time working ON it."

Working smarter means you need to spend more time working ON your business. Too many businesses owners get caught up working in their business, both as a technician or dealing with the day-to-day operations. Worse than that, they end up constantly "fighting fires", never able to gain much traction in moving the business forward.

If you keep doing what you've always done, you'll keep getting the same results. I'm going to introduce you to some simple marketing strategies that direct your efforts to working ON your business, doing things that will make it more successful and capable of growth. If you want to get improved results, you're going to have to make some changes. *Maximizing Business Growth* will guide you through making changes that will produce real and measurable results in your growth and profitability.

MAXIM 3: MARKETING IS AN INVESTMENT

Let's start with the most fundamental question one could ask about business, and that is, "What is the purpose of a business?" Here's how the "father of modern management" and perhaps the most important business mind of the 20th century answers that question:

> "Because its purpose is to create a customer, a business has two basic functions: Marketing and innovation. Marketing and innovation produce results, all the rest are costs."
>
> **Peter Drucker**

Okay, so what exactly is marketing? If you look at 10 different sources, you'll probably get as many different definitions. So let's not focus on the definition of marketing; rather, let's focus on the role of marketing in a business.

The purpose of marketing is to introduce and sell a company's products and services to new, present and past customers.

A business that is effective at marketing has the ability to consistently and repeatedly get customers and clients to purchase their products and services. They can sell and extract as much profit as ethically possible out of each customer over the lifetime of their relationship.

The number one priority of any business should be marketing. If you get down to the bare essentials of business you end up with this: With no new or repeat business, you'll soon be out of business.

Smart marketing is an investment in the growth of your business, and should be treated as one.

MAXIM 4: YOU'RE IN THE MARKETING BUSINESS

This chapter is about creating the proper mindset to grow your business, and there is nothing more important to understand than this…

No matter what business you think you're in, you are actually in the marketing business.

Think about it this way: if nobody is buying what you have to offer, you're not really in business… or you won't be for very long.

This simple concept is vital to your business growth, because until it is internalized and becomes part of your business philosophy, your business will be no better or different than any other business your prospects could choose.

Marketing should focus on all aspects of creating and maintaining customers and clients, and to limit your perspective of marketing to lead generation, customer acquisition, advertising, or sales is a major failure. So many companies separate sales and marketing, often with the two departments not even talking to each other. Selling is part of the marketing process, so never make the mistake of separating the two.

MAXIM 5: CREATE MAXIMUM MARKETING SYNERGY

One of your primary objectives in planning your marketing efforts should be to create the maximum amount of marketing synergy as possible. The next chapter of this book covers this topic in detail, so I will only touch briefly on it here.

Marketing synergy is created when you have marketing tools in place to assist all the marketing functions of your business and all Nine Growth Keys. The TriFecta Exponential Growth Model will help you create a comprehensive marketing program designed to achieve maximum marketing synergy and growth results. It is through marketing synergy that true geometric and exponential growth is realized.

MAXIM 6: TAKE ACTION

Ideas are powerful, and good ideas are extremely important for any business. But as the old adage goes, it's not what you *know*, it's what you *do* that counts.

Ideas keep your business fresh and moving forward. When put into action, good ideas will make a tremendous impact in the growth results you achieve, the way you do business and the fun you have being in business.

This book is full of practical and usable ideas that have made a huge difference for hundreds of businesses, and they'll make a difference for yours, too. But it's up to you to tailor them to your own unique situation and put them into action.

As you read or hear about ideas (not only from this book, but from anywhere), don't make the mistake that too many people make by casting them aside too quickly. Just because you've heard the idea before or it doesn't sound good to you, that doesn't mean it won't do wonders for your business.

Instead, ask yourself the following:

- If you've heard an idea before: Are you using it? Have you ever tried it? If not, why not?
- If you're currently using the idea: How effectively are you using the idea? How can you improve on it to make it more effective for you and your business?
- What will you do as a result of what you've learned?

Ideas have value, but it requires action to realize that value.

MAXIM 7: USE ONLY DIRECT RESPONSE MARKETING

If your goal is to grow your business and produce measurable results with your marketing, then you must only use direct response marketing. I have dedicated Chapter 16 of this book on the topic of direct response marketing.

Direct response marketing and advertising is designed to elicit a specific response from your target audience. These responses can be measured, allowing you to hold direct response marketing activities accountable for producing results.

MAXIM 8: TEST EVERYTHING AND MEASURE RESULTS

Testing is essential for maximizing profits and cutting marketing losses. This is such an important concept, yet it is ignored by most businesses and marketing professionals.

Always test small before committing major funds to any product or marketing activity.

Media advertising reps will offer you a discounted rate to run an ad multiple times. Don't ever agree to do this with a new, unproven advertisement. Always invest a few extra dollars upfront to run it once and see how it performs.

If the advertisement works the first time it runs, then it will work again and you'll recover the money you spent on the test. But what happens if the ad fails multiple times? There's nothing you can do but take a huge loss. That multiple run discount doesn't sound like such a good deal anymore, does it?

Failure to test is most often the result of a mistaken line of thinking from the business owner or executive making the marketing decisions. They think they know what the customer wants, often assuming they know better than their customers. It is very important that you understand this: You can't tell the market what to do. The market tells you what you need to do.

Here's a wonderful quote by one of the most innovative minds in the history of American business:

> "You don't build it for yourself. You find out what the people want and then you build it for them."
>
> **Walt Disney**

The majority of entrepreneurs and business executives I know have larger than average egos. When building a business a large ego is usually a positive attribute. In marketing it can often be detrimental to success.

Your market has the money, and the only vote that counts is the one they make with their wallets. Don't let yourself fall in love with your own ideas, and don't make the mistake of entirely trusting your own judgment.

Test every ad, sales letter, promotion, and every product. Test small and then expand if it is working. Almost all marketing activities can be tested at a safe and low cost level. It doesn't make sense to invest a ton of money in a marketing campaign that may or may not work.

It is simple logic: You don't know what will produce the best results until you test.

Condition yourself to think in terms of marketing tests, not marketing successes or failures. Test fast and cheap, drop poor performing campaigns quickly, then move on to the next test. Ultimately, this is the only way to determine if you have a good idea or not.

If you are truly committed to efficiently growing your business and capturing market share from your competitors, make continual testing a regular part of your marketing.

MAXIM 9: LOOK TO OTHER INDUSTRIES FOR IDEAS

Maybe you're familiar with early self-help pioneer Earl Nightingale. In his book, "Lead the Field", Nightingale makes a very powerful statement that can be directly applied to marketing:

> "If you have no successful example to follow in whatever endeavor you choose, you may simply look at whatever everyone else around you is doing and do the opposite, because the majority is always wrong."
>
> **Earl Nightingale**

He touches on two important points in this statement. The first is to look for successful models and examples to follow. Borrow and emulate the already proven ideas and campaigns you see. Not only is it much faster than creating a campaign from scratch, but you are much more likely to see successful results when you emulate a previously successful campaign.

Perhaps you've heard the old saying, "Pioneers are the ones that get arrows in their backs." This is probably more true in marketing than in the western migration of early America. Why risk failure when you can emulate success?

The second important point to note is that the overwhelming majority of marketing within an industry is almost identical to all the other marketing within that industry. There is no differentiation and everyone looks the same. It's the "Me Too" marketing practice that we discussed in the introduction of this book, and it doesn't work.

Think about it: How can you ever be exceptional when you're the same as everyone else?

When creating marketing campaigns for your business, very rarely will you find the basis for a breakthrough from within your own industry or profession. The real breakthroughs come from the outside. If you want ideas that will differentiate your business from the rest of the mindless sheep following the herd, look to industries other than your own.

MAXIM 10: DEVELOP THE PERSONAL TRAITS OF TOP BUSINESS BUILDERS

Have you ever seen people who succeed in the most impossible conditions? Or maybe you've seen just the opposite: people who have everything going for them but still manage to fail. Very often it's not the idea or the business that makes the difference, it's the person.

The most successful entrepreneurs and business people I know are generally more assertive and creative in making decisions. They don't spend their business lives in reaction mode; they are much more proactive and make things happen.

In my local marketplace in Baton Rouge, LA, there are two entrepreneurs I know that really make things happen. One is a restaurateur, and the other provides a medical service.

You see the restaurateur everywhere. He's involved in every media in town, from local magazines to cable television. He also regularly conducts special events that drive publicity. From a marketing perspective he really makes things happen, and as a result, his establishment is always busy. One night when I was in his restaurant I asked about his marketing activities and what worked best for him. He told me that he tries just about every marketing opportunity he can, and he keeps doing what works.

As far as I can tell, he doesn't have any tracking mechanisms in place, so I doubt he really knows what is working and what is not. The point is that he's proactive and he understands the importance of marketing. I imagine he would be much more successful if he learned to use direct response principles in all of his marketing activities.

The medical service provider appears to have the same approach toward marketing his practice, but it's a little more sophisticated. This business also uses a wide mix of media, from television and radio, to billboards and multiple print media ranging from magazines and newspaper inserts to direct mail co-ops. In most of the marketing I've seen, he also uses a direct response element which allows it to be measured and tracked. I don't know this business owner very well, but I understand his practice has grown dramatically over the past few years.

It is incredible what an open mind, a proactive approach, and the power of direct marketing can do for a business.

OTHER TRAITS OF SUCCESSFUL ENTREPRENEURS AND MARKETERS

There are many other traits found in successful entrepreneurs and marketers, and I would like to touch on a few of them. Even though you may not have all of these traits yourself, most can be learned with practice.

GOAL ORIENTED AND RESULTS FOCUSED

Too many people waste years in their business without understanding what they really *want* from their business. Top entrepreneurs and marketers are the opposite: they are constantly striving to reach their goals, making adjustments and measuring progress along the way.

We've already mentioned that, according to Michael Gerber in his book *"The E-Myth"*, most business owners work so hard in their business that they don't have time to work on their business. As a result, they have become slaves to their business. They basically become employees working for their business rather than their business working for them.

Take your time to analyze and understand where you came from, where you are now, and what you want to accomplish in your business. Set meaningful goals that will help you achieve your objectives. There's truth in that old saying that if you don't know where you want to go, then you'll have no idea of how to get there.

Meaningful goals are essential to your success in business. They give you a target to aim for, a direction to travel, and a purpose for being. Without a clear focus on your goals, it's easy to wander aimlessly and get sidetracked with every little distraction that comes along.

Some time back I was introduced to the acronym "SMART" as it relates to one's goals. Goals should be:

- **Specific** – Know what you're shooting for. Your goals should be clearly defined so you know what you're trying to accomplish and when you achieve it.
- **Measureable** – There should be a system or method of determining how you are progressing in your efforts.
- **Attainable** – If your goal is too high and there is little hope that you reach it, it won't take long for you to become discouraged and lose the drive necessary to achieve the goal.
- **Realistic** – Your goals must be within your realm of achievement or you will become frustrated and give up. Being realistic in your expectations is a key to being good at setting and achieving goals.
- **Time-bound** – you should set a time limit for the attainment of your goals. This keeps you from getting distracted and encourages you to complete what you've started. This is especially important with large goals. Large goals become much more manageable when they're broken down into small goals, each with its own deadline placed on it.

ABILITY TO FOCUS AND STAY ON TARGET

Some people think successful business people must have unique capabilities that others don't have. In my experience, the main difference in successful business people is that they have developed the ability to focus and stay on track. A person of average intelligence who is focused on a clearly defined goal will consistently outperform the brightest people who aren't focused on anything specific.

PERSISTENCE, COMMITMENT AND DETERMINATION

Make a total commitment to your success, and don't let anything hold you back. Decide that you are going to succeed... no matter what.

> "Success is almost totally dependent upon drive and persistence. The extra energy required to make another effort or try another approach is the secret of winning."
>
> **Dennis Waitley**

SELF-RESPONSIBILITY

You are totally responsible for the success of your business and your life. There are no excuses. There will be set-backs and problems that affect your success; many beyond your control. It's up to you to accept responsibility for your success. Always remember, there are many other people who have had greater difficulties than you are ever likely to encounter, and they somehow managed to get through. You can do the same.

CONTROL YOUR TIME

Time is an expendable commodity with each of us getting the same 24 hours each day. When those hours are gone they can never be replaced. You must treat your time as precious and not let anyone disrupt you or take away your focus. If you let others draw you away from your goals, you are accepting that their goals are more important than your own.

FORESIGHT

The ability to look at the past along with what is happening today, and predict what may happen in the future can have a significant impact on your business success. This skill is called foresight.

As a business owner or executive, you should give serious thought to keeping abreast of industry changes, new laws, buying trends, and other factors that could affect your customers, both positively and negatively. Take whatever steps are necessary to prepare yourself to address those changes, and position yourself in the minds of your market as the expert or business they can depend on to help them with these changes.

COMMUNICATION SKILLS

Fortune 1000 executives consistently rate communication skills as the most important skill required to succeed in business. The ability to interact with others on their level so they understand the points you are trying to convey can make or break a business person. Everyone has different communication and behavioral styles; you need to be versatile enough to relate to each person according to their individual style.

SELLING SKILLS

Selling is one of the most important skills a business person can possess. You owe it to yourself and your customers to be the most effective salesperson possible. Even if you're not a full-time sales professional, as a business leader or entrepreneur you are always selling your ideas, your company, and your initiatives. Do yourself a favor and commit to becoming the best salesperson you can be.

Chapter 3:

Understanding Business Growth

Regardless of what you believe or have heard, building a successful business that holds a dominant position in your marketplace doesn't have to be as difficult or costly as many people think it is. Even though today's business environment is more competitive than ever before, there is also more opportunity. The key to capitalizing on that opportunity is understanding and putting into action a few vital business development principles and marketing concepts.

These concepts are universal, so it doesn't matter if your business is a large corporation or a single-operator, home-based business. These simple and logical principles will give you an incredible advantage in your marketplace.

In this chapter I am going to introduce you to one of the single most powerful forces in achieving incredible and exponential growth for your business... even during a slow economy or recession. You will see for yourself that these concepts are easy to understand and implement in any business.

So keep your mind open to the incredible possibilities and let's get started.

HOW BUSINESSES GROW

The first key to maximizing the growth of your business is to understand how your business actually grows, and put this knowledge to use for your advantage.

When you break it down to its simplest elements, everything you do to grow your business can be classified under three primary growth categories. I call this the TriFecta of Business Growth.

You may be familiar with the term "trifecta" as it is used when betting on the horses. A trifecta in horse racing is a special type of bet that is difficult to win but yields very high returns. To win the trifecta bet you must specify which horses will finish in the top three spots and the exact order in which they finish.

Just as in horse racing, where winning the trifecta produces a very high payday, putting the trifecta to work in growing your business will do the same. There is, however, one big difference: winning the trifecta in business is much easier to do... and it doesn't require any luck.

Putting the TriFecta of Business Growth to work for your business will give you an incredible advantage over your competitors. Along with the knowledge and tools you need to create your growth machine, this book provides an easy-to-follow model simplifying the steps you need to take to grow your business in sales, profits and market share.

LINEAR GROWTH

Ask almost any business owner for a description of their marketing activities or a copy of their marketing plan and you'll find that their efforts are most often focused on one activity: lead generation. Lead generation can be conducted via many different media and methods, and the primary goal is to find prospective customers for the business. Although getting new customers is necessary for any business to survive, it is almost always the most expensive form of marketing, and it is not the only goal your marketing should try to accomplish.

Linear Growth occurs when a business falls into the habit of limiting its growth to a singular growth category. This is usually caused by the owner or executive team having a limited view and understanding of marketing.

The majority of companies, including the majority of your competitors, only focus on one growth method (lead generation) to increase their number of customers. If you increase the number of leads for a business by 10%, the business grows by 10%.

LINEAR GROWTH THROUGH IMPROVED LEAD GENERATION

	Leads Generated	Conversion Ratio	New Customers
Current	1000	20%	200
Linear Growth of 10%	1100	20%	220
Actual Growth Achieved			10%

In the above example, our fictitious company started with 1000 leads and closed 20% for a total of 200 new customers. If they were to improve the number of leads generated by 10% while maintaining a conversion ratio of 20%, they end up with 220 new customers. The result is Linear Growth of 10%.

LINEAR GROWTH THROUGH IMPROVED CONVERSION

This same rate of Linear Growth can be achieved by increasing conversion rates by 10%; from 20% to 22%.

	Leads Generated	Conversion Ratio	New Customers
Current	1000	20%	200
Linear Growth of 10%	1000	22%	220
Actual Growth Achieved			**10%**

Dynamic business growth cannot flow out of this limiting, linear approach. To achieve greater growth results you need to have a multi-dimensional approach.

*** A SPECIAL NOTE ON EXAMPLES

Throughout this book I use 10% improvements as the standard for the examples and demonstrations I provide. This is done for two primary reasons:

1. 10% improvements are easy to calculate.
2. 10% is a realistic number. Had I chosen to use larger numbers, such as 20% improvements, the results would be much more dramatic. I use 10% because it is usually an easily attainable goal when improving each of the Nine Growth Keys.

THE TRIFECTA OF BUSINESS GROWTH

As noted earlier, there are only three ways to grow any business, and I call this concept the TriFecta of Business Growth. The three primary growth categories are:

1. Increase the number of customers.
2. Increase the average transaction value.
3. Increase customer purchase frequency.

Let's take a closer look at each of these three parts of the TriFecta of Business Growth.

INCREASE THE NUMBER OF CUSTOMERS

The category of the TriFecta of Business Growth is to increase your number of customers. When more people buy from you, your business grows and you make more money. It's in this growth area that most businesses, including your competition, focus most of their time and marketing dollars.

If you've been in business any length of time, you probably realize that acquiring new customers isn't always the easiest or most profitable thing you can do, and it's almost always the most expensive component of your marketing mix.

Every business, association or professional practice needs new customers and clients; they wouldn't survive without them. However, few businesses really understand what has to happen to get new customers to purchase from them.

Let's take a look at this category of business growth at a deeper level. You see, there are several marketing functions involved in the process of producing new customers, and they may differ from business to business. The most common functions include lead generation, prospect education, and prospect conversion (or closing customers). All of these processes are important, but for many small and mid-sized businesses, lead generation is the only purpose of their marketing. I hope this is not the case for you. If it is, after reading this book and learning the secrets of maximizing business growth, you will do something to remedy that problem.

What is the typical sequence of events that must take place in your business for you to create a new customer? You may find an additional step in your Customer Generation Process, and that's not a problem. The important thing to understand is that you must identify these steps and lead your prospects through the entire process.

Lead Generation and Customer Generation are not the same. Lead Generation is the process of producing a prospective or potential customer for your business. Customer Generation is when that prospect is converted to a paying customer.

Too many businesses never reach their potential because prospects and customers fall through the holes in their marketing process. Don't let this happen to you.

INCREASE THE AVERAGE TRANSACTION VALUE

Getting new customers is important to every business, but there are two more categories of business growth you need to understand. The growth categories of increasing average transaction values and increasing purchase frequency are usually more profitable, more effective, and give you greater potential for leverage than increasing new customers.

The second category of the TriFecta of Business Growth is to increase your customer's average transaction value, or to get your customers to spend more money every time they buy from you. This is one of the most effective ways to increase profits.

When working with new businesses, I find it staggering how many business owners have expensive plans to generate new customers, but very few have paid much attention to the highly profitable step of increasing the size of the average transaction.

Here is an example most of us are familiar with. The fast food industry has completely embraced this concept of increasing the value of the average transaction.

Think about the last time you went through a fast food drive-through – you drive up, place your order, then a voice comes back over the speaker and asks, "Would you like fries or a drink with that?" This is an example of a cross-sell, or selling an additional product along with the original purchase.

Maybe they suggest you super-size your order. This is an example of an up-sell, or increasing the size of the initial order. In either case, if you take them up on one of their offers, what they have done is substantially increase their profits. They have increased their sale and there were no customer acquisition or marketing costs associated with it.

The owners and managers of the fast food restaurants understand that a certain percentage of their customers will say "yes" to their up-sells and cross-sells, and the only reason they say yes is because a suggestion was made to them. It is a numbers game, and those numbers become predictable increases in profits every single day.

But cross-selling and up-selling aren't the only techniques these savvy marketers use to increase the average customer transaction value. They are also experts at a technique called packaging, or bundling. This is when they combine a drink and fries, or maybe a cookie or toy with the order and call it a combo or a Happy Meal.

The customer benefits because they pay less for the package than those items purchased separately would cost; the business benefits because the total purchase amount is higher. Since there were no marketing costs involved, the only cost being for the cost of goods sold, much more profit goes straight to the bottom line.

There are many opportunities for just about every business to increase the average transaction value, the challenge is finding them and making it happen. Later in this book I will get into more detail about this process and how to use it to your advantage. For now I want you to understand that growing your business is not a one-dimensional, "get more customers" initiative. Putting the TriFecta of Business Growth to work for you is easy... so keep reading.

INCREASE CUSTOMER PURCHASE FREQUENCY

The third category of the TriFecta of Business Growth is to increase your customer purchase frequency, or to get your customers to purchase from you more often.

Think of Customer Purchase Frequency like this: the longer customers go between purchases from you, the greater chance they have of buying from your competition. I'm sure you're familiar with the saying "out of sight, out of mind"; well that couldn't be more true than it is in business.

In fact, for every month that your customers do not have meaningful contact with your business, you lose about 10% of your "top-of-mind" awareness. That means that in less than a year you can be completely forgotten, and you cannot afford to let this happen in your business.

You need to have a plan to constantly stay in front of your customers with information they will care about and value. This can range from early notice of sales and special promotions, to announcements and explanations of new products and services, to other offers and information that would benefit them. Your goal is to bond with your prospects and customers while leading them to believe that your solution is perfect for them.

The key is to be fun and to lead them to believe that they would be foolish to do business with anyone other than you.

Think about this concept for your business... What could you do to endear your customers to you? What could you do to lock them into doing business with you while keeping them away from your competition? What could you do to get them coming back more often? What are you doing now? Do you have an educational newsletter? Do you send personal letters via mail? Do you use email? Do you have a website that keeps them abreast of what's new?

Here is another important question you need to know the answer to: How long, on average, do the customers who buy from you remain your customers? How long do they continue to do business with you before they move on? Are they one-time buyers, or do they stay with you for a year, two years, five years, or ten years?

Your marketing plan needs to contain strategic systems to not only keep your customers coming back, but to keep them coming back forever. If it doesn't, you are losing more customers each year to your competition than you have to.

PUTTING IT ALL TOGETHER

All business growth can be categorized under the TriFecta of Business Growth: Increase the number of customers, increase average transaction values, and increase customer purchase frequency. To maximize the growth of your business, the goal of your marketing program should be to improve all three of the primary growth categories simultaneously. When you do this, something amazing happens – you begin to create Marketing Synergy, and that gives a tremendous advantage in building and growing your business. And it's an advantage that very few businesses have working for them.

You may be familiar with the often used business term of synergy. Dictionary.com defines synergy as *"the interaction of two or more agents or forces so that their combined effect is greater than the sum of their individual effects."*

The definition of Marketing Synergy is very similar: *"The principle in marketing that the whole is greater than the sum of the parts; putting the marketing mix variables together in a way that achieves maximum effect."*

When your marketing efforts focus on improving your business in all three growth categories, you create Marketing Synergy and move beyond Linear Growth to Geometric Growth.

To demonstrate Linear Growth, let's create another fictitious business using some simple numbers. Suppose you have a business with 1000 customers spending an average of $100 per purchase, and buying from you an average of 10 times per year. What you end up with is $1,000,000 per year in revenues.

Now imagine that you were able to improve each of the three primary growth areas by 10%. You would then have 1100 customers spending $110 per transaction, buying 11 times each year. Your total revenues would jump to $1,331,000 per year, which is a total of 33.1%.

THE TRIFECTA OF BUSINESS GROWTH – 10% IMPROVEMENTS

	Number of Customers	Average Transaction Value	Yearly Purchase Frequency	Gross Sales
Now	1000	100	10	$1,000,000
+10%	1100	110	11	$1,331,000
			Actual Growth Achieved	**33.1%**

Through Marketing Synergy the total growth is greater than the sum of the three growth categories. Instead of 10% + 10% + 10% = 30%, the total growth increases to 33.1%. Marketing Synergy gives us a growth bonus of 3.1%! This is called Geometric Growth.

> **Note**: In the preceding examples I use improvements of 10% to make the calculations simple and the growth improvements realistic. With a well-executed marketing program, these numbers could be higher.

THE TRIFECTA OF BUSINESS GROWTH – 20% IMPROVEMENTS

	Number of Customers	Average Transaction Value	Yearly Purchase Frequency	Gross Sales
Now	1000	100	10	$1,000,000
+20%	1200	120	12	$1,728,000
			Actual Growth Achieved	**72.8%**

In this example, 20% + 20% +20% doesn't equal 60%, it totals an incredible growth of 72.8%. Can you see the synergistic effect that's going on here? The total growth of the business is much greater than the sum of each of the growth areas by a total of 12.8 percentage points. That is a significant amount of "bonus" growth, and that is the power of putting Geometric Growth to work for your business.

How can Marketing Synergy affect the overall growth of your company? To maximize growth potential, management should always focus on the TriFecta of Business Growth.

THE NINE GROWTH KEYS

In the previous section we learned that all business growth falls under three primary categories, which I call the TriFecta of Business Growth. Now I want to take the concept of creating Marketing Synergy to an even higher, more powerful and more exciting level. When put into action in your business, this concept gives you astounding growth results. I call this the Nine Growth Keys.

Let me ask you a question: How many different ways do you think there are to grow a business? You may be surprised to learn that all business growth can be categorized under nine specific areas, and I call these the Nine Growth Keys.

To maximize your business growth, your marketing efforts should focus on improving all Nine Growth Keys. By effectively accomplishing this with your marketing, you'll gain incredible control over your sales and marketing processes. Not only does this get you infinitely closer to reaching your growth potential, it can be done more quickly than you might imagine.

1. **Lead Generation** – getting individuals or companies to express interest in your products or services.
2. **Prospect Conversion** – turning a lead into a customer or client; also known as closing the deal.
3. **Customer Reactivation** – getting dormant customers to purchase from you again.
4. **Referral Generation** – when a person or business is directed to another business via an existing customer.
5. **Size of Purchase** – the dollar value of the transaction.
6. **Profit Margins** – the ratio of profitability calculated as net profits divided by sales; how much out of every dollar of sales a company actually keeps in earnings.
7. **Number of Customer Purchases** – number of occasions during a period of time that a buyer purchases from a particular seller.
8. **Customer Buying Lifetime** – extend the average period of time a customer or client does business with a particular company.
9. **Reducing Customer Attrition** – reduce the loss of clients or customers to a business; also known as customer churn, customer turnover, or customer defection. This is the opposite of Customer Retention.

The first five growth keys are Growth Multipliers because these factors can be multiplied together to significantly improve business growth. The last four growth keys are Growth Magnifiers. Improving the Growth Magnifiers strengthens results produced by the Growth Multipliers.

If your goal is to maximize the growth of your business, you must strive to make continual improvements to each of these Nine Growth Keys. When you do, you generate tremendous Marketing

Synergy, and you are on your way toward achieving exponential growth.

There are literally hundreds of marketing strategies and tools you can apply toward improving each of the Nine Growth Keys. I will cover some of the most effective ones in upcoming chapters of this book. It is important for you to understand that your marketing efforts must focus on improving all Nine Growth Keys if you want to maximize your growth potential.

THE LAW OF COMPOUNDING

One of the most important principles for maximizing business growth is the Law of Compounding.

Albert Einstein is often quoted as saying something to the effect of "compounding is the most powerful force in the universe." It is unknown whether or not Einstein actually said this, but if he didn't, maybe he should have.

Compounding is most often referred to in the context of investing as compound interest. Investopedia.com defines compounding as *"the ability of an asset to generate earnings, which are then reinvested in order to generate earnings from previous earnings."*

In the context of business growth, compounding is a bit different, though the effects can be just as dramatic. By making a series of small, incremental changes to specific and interrelated elements of a business (The Nine Growth Keys), a business can achieve incredible growth very quickly.

If your business goal is to double your profits the Law of Compounding can make this much easier to accomplish than you might think. By making 10% improvements to the five Growth Multipliers, you will improve your profits by 61.05%.

To clearly illustrate the power of the Law of Compounding, let's improve five of the Nine Growth Keys by 10%. These Growth Keys act as growth multipliers to increase the profits of this fictitious business by over 61%.

THE LAW OF COMPOUNDING IN BUSINESS GROWTH

	Now	+10%
Leads Generated	5000	5500
Conversion Rate	20%	22%
Total Number of Sales Closed	**1,000**	**1,210**

Yearly Purchases per Customer	10	11
Total Number of Purchases	**10,000**	**13,310**

Size of Purchase	$ 100	$ 110
Total Gross Sales	**$ 1,000,000**	**$1,464,100.00**

Profit Margins	50%	55%
Total Profits	**$ 500,000**	**$ 805,255**

By making 10% increases in the five Growth Keys, our business was able to make the following improvements:

Increased Sales:	**46.41%**
Increased Profits:	**61.05%**

All the Growth Keys in this example are interrelated and work together to activate the Law of Compounding in this example. An increase in the number of leads generated compounds on top of the increase in conversion. In turn, the higher number of closed sales compounds on top of the increased yearly purchases per customer. An increase in the size of your average sales transaction compounds on top of the previous increases, as does an increase of your profit margins.

Keep in mind that you don't have to make improvements in each of the Growth Keys all at once. They can be done in sequence over time, with the effect of one change compounding on top of the previous change. The example above shows how relatively small changes in your business can add up to substantial business growth, dramatically increasing sales and profits over a relatively short period of time.

When you put Marketing Synergy and the Law of Compounding to work for your business, you gain the ability to grow to levels you may never have deemed attainable.

Chapter 4:

The TriFecta Exponential Growth Model

In the previous chapter you were introduced to several important business development principles that, when put into action will accelerate and multiply your success. As a quick review, these principles are:

The TriFecta of Business Growth – all business growth falls under one of three primary categories:

1. Increase the number of customers.
2. Increase the average transaction value.
3. Increase customer purchase frequency.

The Nine Growth Keys exist within the TriFecta of Business Growth and enable business leaders and marketers to further break down the growth of a business.

Five of the Growth Keys are **Growth Multipliers**:

1. Lead Generation
2. Prospect Conversion
3. Average Transaction Value
4. Profit Margins
5. Frequency of Purchase

Four of the Growth Keys are **Growth Magnifiers**:

6. Referral Generation
7. Reduced Customer Attrition
8. Customer Reactivation
9. Extend Customer's Buying Lifetime

Marketing Synergy is created when your marketing efforts are put together in a way that complement one another and produces maximum effect.

The Law of Compounding allows us to make a series of small, incremental changes to specific and interrelated elements of a business (The Nine Growth Keys) to achieve incredible growth very quickly.

Now we are going to put all of these potent principles into a model that can explode the growth of your business.

THE TRIFECTA EXPONENTIAL GROWTH MODEL

The secret to maximizing your business success lies in learning how to grow your business effectively. There are many factors that attribute to a company's success, such as reputation, location, current marketing and advertising activities, etc. Your goal as a business owner or executive is to make all of these factors work for you in an advantageous and beneficial way, creating as much momentum and Marketing Synergy as possible.

That is where the TriFecta Exponential Growth Model comes in. Once you learn how to use the model, you will spend less time, money and effort in your sales and marketing activities, yet the results will eclipse any others you have ever produced. Just like the purpose of this book, the TriFecta Exponential Growth Model is completely focused on creating real results of increased sales, profits and market share.

The TriFecta Exponential Growth Model is not a business strategy within itself, but it will help you think more strategically about your business. As long as your business strategy involves growing, the TriFecta Exponential Growth Model makes achieving growth considerably easier. Businesses with limited marketing and sales resources will realize new potential to maximize growth without dramatically increasing marketing costs.

I've been advising business owners on how to grow their companies faster and more profitably for 15 years. Of the hundreds of companies I've worked with, some were Fortune 500 corporations, but most were entrepreneurial companies ranging from zero-revenue start-ups to companies that produced tens of millions of dollars in revenues in just a couple of years. The TriFecta Exponential Growth Model has worked for every single company that has ever applied it.

MARKETING IS LEADERSHIP

Successfully marketing a business requires leadership. Not the type of leadership that you are probably thinking about, which is providing internal vision, direction and motivation for your employees, investors and vendors. Obviously this type of leadership is important, but it's not what this book is about.

The type of leadership I am referring to is customer leadership. Customer leadership is simply taking the responsibility and appropriate actions to lead your customers and prospects through the process of doing business with you, over and over again. This process includes everything from creating motivational marketing messages and convincing prospects to buy, to building long-term relationships, and ultimately getting your customers to tell others about you. Your marketing programs must take full responsibility for leading your target market through this entire process.

ACHIEVING EXPONENTIAL GROWTH

Exponential Growth occurs when subtle improvements to sales and marketing results combine to dramatically impact the bottom line of a business.

The concept of Exponential Growth is incredible, and it is not just theory. Smart marketers, entrepreneurs and business leaders have been using these principles for years, and this type of growth is attainable for almost any established small or mid-sized business. The key is that you must approach it from an intelligent and comprehensive marketing perspective.

UNDERSTANDING THE TRIFECTA EXPONENTIAL GROWTH MODEL

The first column of the model represents how the majority of marketing plans are implemented, with a single focus of generating leads. A 10% improvement in lead generation equals a 10% growth in the company. This is Linear Growth.

The second column of the model puts the TriFecta of Business Growth to work for your business. You begin to achieve Marketing Synergy when you simultaneously improve all three growth categories (number of customers, average transaction value, customer purchase frequency). Improvement of 10% in each of these three categories results in a total of 33.1% growth, with Marketing Synergy producing "bonus" growth of 3.1 percentage points for your business.

TriFecta Exponential Growth Model

Linear Growth	Geometric Growth	The Nine Growth Keys of Exponential Growth	
	Number of Customers	1. Lead Generation	+10%
		2. Prospect Conversion	+10%
		3. Customer Reactivation	+10%
Linear Business Growth	+10%	4. Referrals	+10%
	Average Transaction Value	5. Size of Purchase	+10%
		6. Profit Margins	+10%
	+10%		
	Customer Purchase Frequency	7. Number of Purchases	+10%
		8. Extend Buying Lifetime	+10%
10%	+10%	9. Reduce Customer Attrition	+10%
Linear Growth = 10%	Geometric Growth = 33.1%	Exponential Growth =	?*

* By improving each of the Nine Growth Keys by 10%, exponential growth results can total 120% or more!

The third column gets even more exciting. When you improve each of the Nine Growth Keys, you are fully utilizing the Law of Compounding in growing your business, creating maximum Marketing Synergy. Improving each of the Nine Growth Keys by 10% will grow your profits by 123% or more! That's the incredible power of the TriFecta Exponential Growth Model when implemented fully.

In the previous chapter we reviewed what the Law of Compounding could accomplish when utilizing five of the Growth Keys in your marketing efforts. A 10% increase in each of the five Growth Multipliers resulted in a 46.41% increase in sales, and a 61.05% increase in profits.

A 61% increase in profits is extraordinary considering all we did was increase profit margins by 10% (from 50% to 55%). This type of exponential growth in profitability can only be achieved when your marketing efforts improve all Nine Growth Keys.

Now let's put the entire TriFecta Exponential Growth Model with all Nine Growth Keys to work for this same fictitious business. This will give you a better idea of what the Law of Compounding and Marketing Synergy, when fully implemented, can do to grow your sales and profits. Take a look at the exponential growth calculations on the following page. Once again I'll use 10% as the standard level of improvement for each of the Growth Keys.

EXPONENTIAL GROWTH CALCULATIONS

Growth Multipliers		Current Business	10% Improvement
A	Leads Generated Annually	2,000	2,200
B	Conversion Rate	20%	22%
C	Number of New Customers (A x B)	400	484
D	Average Customer Transactions Per Year	10	11
E	Total Number of Yearly Transactions (C x D)	4,000	5,324
F	Average Transaction Value	$ 100.00	$ 110
G	Total Sales (E x F)	$ 400,000.00	$ 585,640
H	Profit Margins	50%	55%
I	Total Profits (G x H)	$ 200,000	$ 322,102.00

Growth Magnifiers		Current Business	10% Improvement
J	Referrals Generated Annually	100	110
K	Referral Conversion Rate	30%	33%
L	Number of Referral Customers (J x K)	30	36
M	Total Number of Customers (C x S)	2,000	-----
N	Customer Attrition Rate of 20% (M x 20%)	400	-----
O	Customers from Reduced Attrition (N x 10%)	-----	40
P	Total Inactive Customers (N x 4 yrs.)	1,600	-----
Q	Reactivated Customers (P x 10%)	-----	160
R	Total Regained Customers (O + Q)	-----	200
S	Average Customer Buying Lifetime (in years)	5	5.5
T	Customer Lifetime Value (D x F x S)	$ 5,000	$ 6,655

Exponential Growth Totals		Current Business	10% Improvement
U	Total New Customers (C + L + R)	430	720
V	Total Sales (D x F x U)	$ 430,000	$ 871,563
W	Total Profits (V x H)	$ 215,000	$ 479,360

X	Improvement in New Customers	68%
Y	Improvement in Sales	103%
Z	Improvement in Profits	123%

55

REVIEW OF THE EXPONENTIAL GROWTH CALCULATIONS

The growth calculations on the previous page are results from improving each of the Nine Growth Keys by 10%. To make the calculations easier to follow, I have lettered each of the line items from A – Z. Many calculations are self-explanatory, while others require further explanation to understand fully. Below are several line items revisited in greater detail:

J.   **Referrals Generated Annually** is the total number of leads resulting from referrals during one year.

K.   **Referral Conversion Rate** is the percentage of referral leads that convert to actual paying customers.

M.   **Total Number of Customers** is the total number of active customers that purchase from the business. For this example, I multiplied the Number of New Customers (C.) by the Average Customer Buying Lifetime (S.).

N.   **Customer Attrition Rate** is the percentage of customers a business loses each year (the opposite of Retention Rate). A Customer Attrition Rate of 20% is an average that typically works across most industries.

O.   **Customers from Reduced Attrition** is calculated by taking the number of customers lost to attrition (N.) and reducing it by 10%. The net result is 40 customers "gained" by not losing them to attrition.

P.   **Total Inactive Customers** is calculated by multiplying the annual Customer Attrition Rate of 20% (N.) by 4 years.

Q.   **Reactivated Customers** are the number of Total Inactive Customers (P.) that resume purchasing from the business.

R.   **Total Regained Customers** is a result of adding Reactivated Customers (Q.) to Customers from Reduced Attrition (O.).

The exponential growth resulting from improving all Nine Growth Keys by 10% is astounding. Total new sales grew by

56

103%, and total profits increased by 123%. Considering the logical and systematic approach of the TriFecta Exponential Growth Model, combined with the assistance of Marketing Synergy and the Law of Compounding, the goal of doubling your profits doesn't seem so impossible. It just requires 10% improvements in each of the Nine Growth Keys.

If you are like most entrepreneurs and business executives, you are reading this book and wondering how the TriFecta Exponential Growth Model can be applied to your specific business and your specific situation. That's good, because it is the first step in creating exponential growth in your company.

THE COMPREHENSIVE MARKETING PROGRAM

There's an old advertising saying that I learned when I first started out in marketing that goes something like: "Any fool can make soap, but it takes a clever man to sell it." Would it really matter if you made the best soap on earth if nobody bought it?

Maybe you don't want to think of your business as the maker of just another piece of soap, but that is exactly what it is. There are a thousand others out there that do what you do. You may be an accounting or legal wizard, or the world's greatest widget or mousetrap manufacturer... but so are numerous others whose ads sit right next to yours in the yellow pages and other media.

If you want your business to be successful, you must set yourself apart from all of your competitors and make acquiring and keeping customers and clients your highest priority. It just so happens that getting and maximizing customer value is the purpose of marketing.

It's really important for you to internalize this concept. Suppose you truly came to believe that one of the most important functions of your business is the marketing of your products and services. What would you do differently? Would you prioritize your time differently? Would you change the amount of money you invest in marketing to grow your business?

Believe it or not, most businesses I have evaluated over the years don't have an effective marketing plan, and that's a big mistake. Multiple studies conducted by the SBA have shown that small businesses with a marketing plan consistently outperform competitors without a marketing plan by an average of 30%.

I have found two primary reasons why entrepreneurs and business leaders get into trouble with their marketing efforts:

1. They are choosing the wrong marketing tools and tactics to achieve their goals.
2. They are not using the marketing tools and tactics effectively.

Basically, they are doing the wrong things, and they're doing them the wrong way. Not to sound too obvious, but your goal should be to choose the right marketing tools to achieve your strategic objectives, and to use those tools in the most effective way possible. Basing your marketing plan on the TriFecta Exponential Growth Model will help you achieve this.

Creating an effective marketing plan that will guide and propel your business far ahead of where it is now doesn't have to be a painful experience. You can create a marketing plan in a very short time.

The key to a powerful marketing plan is having an effective marketing strategy and an effective and comprehensive tactical approach toward improving the Nine Growth Keys.

Let's turn our focus to the key word I use to describe the marketing plan, and that is "comprehensive." A Comprehensive Marketing Program is one that takes responsibility for improving all Nine Growth Keys, from lead generation through continually working toward extending your customer's buying lifetime.

A Comprehensive Marketing Program doesn't leave anything out, because when you do, you reduce the effect the Law of Compounding has on your growth, thus destroying the synergy of the model. The goal is to maximize your business growth, and implementing only four or five of the Nine Growth Keys won't get you the best results.

USING MULTIPLE MARKETING TOOLS

There are many different marketing tools and tactics available, and the best marketing programs will have multiple tools working to achieve each one of the growth keys. You cannot rely on just one or two marketing tools for each of the growth keys. If you do, you put the growth and stability of your company at risk.

Here is an example using the growth key of Lead Generation…

Imagine that your business relies on television advertising to generate leads. What would happen if that media no longer produced the same results for you? What if it went out of business, or one of your competitors started buying up huge chunks of air time, greatly reducing your visibility? It would definitely hurt, if not seriously cripple, your business.

When building your business, having a contingency plan is a key to stability. There are many factors in the marketplace that are out of your control. You are dependent upon vendors, media, sales people, et al., and they will fail you from time to time. Not only must you have a contingency plan to deal with these situations, but you need to have multiple marketing tools and systems in place for every marketing function to minimize the effects of these failures.

How many marketing tools are you using now? Many businesses only have a couple of tools working for them, and this could lead to catastrophic failures. Having multiple marketing tools working for you to achieve improvements in each of the Nine Growth Keys is one of the best defenses against marketing disaster.

Many business people have told me that they have tried everything to grow their business, but nothing seems to work. I always respond by asking them what they are doing now, and what they have tried in the past. I think you can see where I'm going with this. Their reply is often something like: "I've tried the Yellow Pages, ran an ad in the paper, and I send out some direct mail letters."

I am not saying you can't have incredible success with any of those activities, because you can. Just think about what you could do by using 5, 10, or 20 more tools to grow your business? What effect would this have if each marketing tool was working for you and producing a positive return on investment? This is the key to creating multiple revenue sources, and it is what every business should strive to achieve.

There are hundreds of different marketing tools and strategies to choose from and put to work for your business. How many are you using to your advantage right now?

When evaluating new marketing opportunities for your business, ask yourself which growth keys the activity will help you improve. Many marketing tools can impact multiple growth keys when used properly. Two that come to mind are sales people and company newsletters.

A sales person can accomplish every growth key on their own. If you don't have other marketing tools supporting the growth and stability of your company, make certain that the duties of your sales people include all Nine Growth Keys.

In the interest of efficiency and effectiveness, I don't recommend this practice. Instead, I suggest using your sales team in the growth keys which they can generate the highest return for your business, and that is to focus on conversion.

Another versatile marketing tool that has incredible utility in marketing is the company newsletter. Through education and follow up, it assists in increasing conversion rates, generating referrals, increasing the frequency of purchases, extending a customer's buying lifetime, reducing customer attrition, and reactivating inactive customers. I highly recommend that every business use a company newsletter.

Achieving maximum growth and stability in your business requires a marketing program utilizing multiple marketing tools constantly improving each of the Nine Growth Keys.

In the city where I live I know of two businesses that are constantly testing new media and marketing opportunities. Their marketing is not the best, and there are many things they could do to improve the results they get, however they do understand the importance of marketing, and they understand the importance of testing new marketing activities. Even though they have immense room for improvement, both of them have the most successful businesses of their category in our local marketplace.

I want to share a metaphor with you that helps illustrate this point: Marketing tools are to business as legs are to stools. One-legged stools fall over. Two-legged stools fall over, too. Three-legged stools will support you, but what if something were to go wrong? What if you leaned over just a little too far in the wrong direction? You could still fall over. What if one of the legs broke? Then you would have a two-legged stool, and we already know what they do.

Four-legged stools are more stable, but if one of the legs were to break, then you've got a three-legged stool once again.

But what if you had a five or six-legged stool? That would be much more stable. What about a seven-legged stool? It would stay up forever.

If you're like many businesses, you're operating with a one or two-legged stool. You think you have a business, but what you really have is a sales force and an advertising campaign. If one of your key sales people were to leave, or if some outside factors harm your advertising efforts, you could be in an awful position.

I'm not saying this will happen to you. What I am saying is that building your business with only one or two marketing tools is a recipe for disaster, and it is just a matter of time until something breaks down.

Build strength and stability into your business by adding multiple tools to each of the Nine Growth Keys.

CONSTANT FORWARD PROGRESS

Maximizing the growth of your business requires you to adopt the mindset of "constant forward progress." You must continually strive to make improvements and gains in all Nine Growth Keys of your business.

Getting started is easier than you think. The first step is to learn to use the TriFecta Exponential Growth Model. Identify the growth keys that you believe will make the most impact on your business. Decide where to start based on two criteria: the areas of greatest potential, and the ease and cost of implementation. What you're looking for is the "low hanging fruit." What is the easiest thing you can do that will make a difference? Do it.

Your results will vary. Maybe you will produce a 10% improvement with your effort; maybe it will be less. Who knows, maybe your business will explode? At this point don't dwell on it, just move on to the next growth key that you think has the most potential and do something to make improvements in that area.

Do something to improve lead generation, and then do something to improve conversion. Do something next month to reactivate inactive customers, then do something to keep them from becoming inactive again. Do something to improve each of the Nine Growth Keys, then start all over again.

Chapter 5:

Thinking Strategically... and Tactically

In my years of business, I've been fortunate enough to see the inner operations of both Fortune 500 companies and small businesses. I've seen the "re-engineering" of operational procedures, supply chain systems, human resources, and product development systems. As interesting as these projects were, none had as much impact on the success of the business as implementing strategic marketing. Strategic marketing grows business, and that's why I love it so much.

Notice that I used the term "strategic marketing" as opposed to just "marketing". Strategic marketing means your efforts must achieve a clearly defined and measureable marketing objective for it to be worthwhile. The success of most marketing efforts cannot be measured at all, therefore they cannot be held accountable for results. As the famous saying goes:

"If you can't measure it, it's not worth doing."

There is also a big difference between strategic and tactical marketing. As we learned in the first chapter, in the last 20 years customer acquisition costs have tripled and marketing effectiveness has been cut in half. There is more competition than ever, it is costing more money to reach your target market, and it is not going to get any easier. You must have a strategic focus to get the most from your marketing efforts and expense.

Business tactics are methods or techniques used in working toward achieving your strategy. Tactics can consist of many different marketing activities, such as running ads and direct mail campaigns to generating leads for your sales force.

A business strategy is a carefully defined and detailed plan to achieve a long-term goal, impact or position in the marketplace. To achieve maximum growth, your marketing program must be designed with your long-term strategy in mind. Tactics should be combined in a way to produce Marketing Synergy while striving to accomplish as many strategic objectives as possible. You must learn to think strategically to do this.

The majority of entrepreneurs, business leaders and marketers are what I call "tactical marketers." Tactical marketers think in terms of generating a lead or making a sale today. They have a limited grasp on strategy. When you tell them that generating a lead is twice as hard as it was 20 years ago, they will think of ways to make the sales team try twice as hard, or make twice as many prospecting calls.

Many entrepreneurs and sales leaders are tactical in nature, realizing that taking action is necessary to achieve success. This drive to take action is a great trait to have, and it will take you far in business. However, when you combine it with the ability to think more strategically, you will achieve far greater results in sales and marketing.

"Strategic marketers" see the situation from a different perspective, creating plans to solve problems that tactical marketers would never develop. While this sounds great, the problem is that most strategic marketers are not very interested in tactics, and as a result, they are not very good at them either. Very often you see wonderful ideas and strategies that never produce results because they fail at implementation.

Execution of your strategy is critical to success in growing your business. The best strategy in the world is of little use if you fail at implementation. Here are a couple of quotes from famous World War II generals that drive this point home:

> "Amateurs study strategy, but professionals study logistics."
>
> **Omar Bradley**
> General of the Army
> First Chairman of the Joint Chiefs of Staff
>
> ---
>
> "A good plan, violently executed now, is better than a perfect plan executed next week."
>
> **General George Patton**

To maximize your business growth, you need to be both a strategic and tactical marketer. You must be able to develop the big ideas and strategy and also implement them at a tactical level with discipline and determination. As a strategist you will look at all the changes in your market environment as opportunities to out-think and out-maneuver your competition. As a tactician you will get out there and make it happen. As both a strategist and a tactician, you will learn how to test and measure the results your efforts produce, constantly making adjustments to improve your efficiency and effectiveness.

STRATEGICALLY FOCUS ON THE NINE GROWTH KEYS

Even though the TriFecta Exponential Growth Model is not a strategy in itself, following it helps you think more strategically about your business.

The core concept of the TriFecta Exponential Growth Model is to maximize the growth of your business by making consistent improvements to the Nine Growth Keys. Because these growth keys interrelate with one another, successful implementation of the model creates Marketing Synergy and activates the Law of Compounding. When you improve the Nine Growth Keys by just 15% each, you can literally double or triple your profitability.

Realistically, that kind of hyper-growth is difficult to manage, and there will be growing pains along the way. That is why it is so important to create marketing "systems" that you can turn on and off as needed. The important thing to understand is that your business will grow, and you will have more control over your growth than ever before.

Working your way through the TriFecta Exponential Growth Model is not something you will do just once. It is something that will become a continual part of your business strategy and operation. You will work through it once, making improvements to each of the Nine Growth Keys, then work through the model again, making more improvements. Each time you work through it you will become more sophisticated as a marketer and business builder, and each time your efforts will build upon your previous efforts and results.

Once you finish implementing one tactic to improve one of the growth keys, choose another growth key and tactic to put into action. This is a continuous improvement strategy that builds exponentially over time. You don't have to be perfect with any single tactic, you can just move on to the next one.

By keeping your marketing efforts directed on the Nine Growth Keys, the TriFecta Exponential Growth Model enables you to achieve incredible Marketing Synergy and growth. As long as the model is aligned with your overall business strategy, it keeps you moving forward toward reaching your goals in sales, profits and market share.

TARGET AND NICHE MARKETS

Just as you can't be all things to all people, you can't market your products and services to everyone, even if you think that everyone needs them. I'm not saying that you can't be successful doing this, but you greatly reduce your efficiency and potential by not focusing on select groups of consumers or businesses. These specific groups are called "niches."

Niche marketing is simply marketing to customer groups that fit the demographic and psychographic profile of your target market, and it represents your best chance of getting a good return on your marketing investment.

To succeed in today's hyper-competitive marketplace, you need to concentrate your marketing resources on smaller, well-chosen segments or niches. By marketing specifically to the needs and requirements of your chosen niche, you are showing them that you are the company that understands them and their situation better than anyone else. You may not get the business of others outside of your targeted niche, but you increase the amount of business you receive from your niche.

Through niche marketing you can become a dominant force because your products and services are seen as "specially designed" to solve the problems of a particular market. The result is higher conversion rates, lower customer acquisition costs, and increased market share in a particular category very quickly.

One of the most common marketing mistakes business leaders make is not focusing on specific niche markets.

BENEFITS OF NICHE MARKETING

People often ask me, "If I limit my market, won't I be reducing my chances of doing business with more customers?"

Yes, but by targeting your marketing to niches you are able to connect with them at much higher levels.

Targeting your market to specific niches accomplishes several important strategic objectives:

- Prospecting becomes easier and less expensive because you can focus your lead generation efforts on media and activities associated with that niche market.
- Your offering becomes more attractive because people better appreciate products and services made specifically for them.
- You generate referrals and create brand recognition more quickly. People in groups communicate with each other. If you're good at providing your product or service to your niche, your name and reputation will spread quickly.

TYPES OF NICHES

There are four basic types of niche markets:

1. **Demographic Niches** consist of people sharing one or more common characteristics.
2. **Psychographic Niches** incorporate the study of how people think and what they like. People with the same psychographic profiles often share the same passions and hobbies. This is perhaps the largest and most lucrative type of niche category because people spend a lot of their discretionary income on things they are passionate about.
3. **Geographic Niches** include people who live in the same areas, such as neighborhoods, zip codes, voting precincts, cities, metropolitan areas, counties, states, etc. These people often share the same problems and need the same products and services as others in their area.
4. **Occupational Niches** consist of people who share the same occupations. Often members of occupational niches share the same problems and concerns, making them good candidates for products and services created to solve the specific problems of the occupation.

SELECTING THE RIGHT NICHE MARKETS

Choosing the right niche market is an important decision that must be researched carefully. Here are several questions you should ask yourself when evaluating and choosing a niche market:

Question 1: Can you easily and affordably contact the niche? Be careful about choosing a niche that doesn't have an association, trade publication, or hold conferences.

Question 2: Can the niche afford your products and services? It doesn't make sense to market to someone who can't afford to buy from you.

Question 3: Is there a successful track record of selling these types of products or services to the niche? A common mistake is to create products that require people to change their normal habits. Old habits die hard, and bringing a new product to a new market is one of the most difficult and expensive marketing endeavors. Pick a niche market that is not only already buying products and services similar to yours, but also paying the prices that you want to charge.

Question 4: How much competition is in the niche? The more competition in the market, the more aggressively you must market to capture market share. This is one of the reasons why your product and service must be unique enough to stand out from the crowd. We'll cover this in greater detail in the next chapter.

Question 5: Is the niche large enough to sustain your business? One of the first calculations you should do when deciding on a niche market is a breakeven assessment, which identifies how much of the market you have to penetrate just to break even. If you must penetrate a high percentage of the market just to break even, you may want to reconsider going into this niche. However, if you can break even by just penetrating a small portion of the market, the niche may be a good one to consider.

Question 6: Do you have experience with the niche? People like to buy from people who understand them and their problems; others who have "been there and done that." Additionally, the more you know about the problems facing your niche customer, the better you can tailor solutions that solve their problems.

NICHE MARKETING FOR ESTABLISHED BUSINESSES

If you have an established business and want to start selling to niche markets, the first step is to review your customer list from the past few years. Based on what you know about them, are there any similarities or trends that you can spot? If so, segment the list based on these identifiable similarities.

From these segmented lists, can you tell if they are the types of people that are proven to buy from you? If so, you will have some degree of certainty that they will be good candidates to purchase your products and services.

REACHING YOUR NICHE

Very often the most difficult step in your niche marketing strategy is finding how to reach them. That's why it is so important to choose a niche market you can easily contact. Any expert direct marketer will tell you that the list is the most important component of a direct marketing campaign. If you cannot easily and affordably contact a niche market, you shouldn't be marketing to it.

The easiest way to find your niche market is to ask yourself a very simple question: "Who else markets to them?" Often these companies will rent you their list or work with you for a "commission" from products or services you sell as a result of using their list.

Other common sources for finding your niche market include:

- Yellow Pages / electronic yellow pages
- Oxbridge Dictionary of Publications
- Standard Rate and Data Service (SRDS) list directory
- Organizations and associations to which your niche market belongs.

- MediaFinder.com to search for magazines, newsletters and other media that are targeted toward your niche.
- Contact a list broker for help.

If you cannot find a list of your target market, then it's up to you to do the lead generation to create your own list.

This marketing process is expensive and time consuming, but you own the list once you build it. Chapter 6 of this book is all about lead generation.

Once you decide to market to a particular niche, you will need marketing tools designed specifically to capture their attention. Every niche has their own "hot buttons", and through your research you should have discovered their frustrations and the language they use in their conversations. You must know this information to create your marketing tools, such as sales letters, advertisements, white papers, press releases, newsletters, websites, and sales presentations.

FIND ANOTHER NICHE

Once you have successfully penetrated one niche, you can easily apply what you have learned to entering another niche.

A great example are the *"Chicken Soup for the Soul"* books. The book is cross-niched into dozens of different niche markets. There may be dozens of niche markets available to you, too.

WHAT ARE YOUR CUSTOMERS WORTH?

One of the most important things you could ever understand about your business is how much revenue and profit your average customer is worth during their "buying lifetime" with your company. This critical concept is called Lifetime Customer Value, and it can have an enormous impact on your business.

Lifetime Customer Value is the average profit a customer generates over the duration of their relationship with a business.

By knowing your Lifetime Customer Value, you can determine how much you can afford to spend to acquire new customers, and how much you can afford to spend to keep your existing customers from leaving you for your competition.

The easiest way to explain this concept is to give an example. To attract new customers a retail store runs an advertisement that costs $1,500. The ad generates 10 new customers that purchase an average of $100 each, totaling $1,000 in new sales.

The store interprets the results of the promotion as $1,500 ad cost minus $1,000 in sales, equals a $500 loss. They conclude that the advertisement didn't work for them... and that's a big mistake.

The retail store is failing to see the future opportunity for more purchases. If this store has great products and good customer service, let's say, on average, those 10 new customers come back twice a year and spend $100 each time. On top of that, let's assume that they will continue doing business with this store for an average of 5 years each. Now we're looking at 20 return visits and purchases for $100 each, or a total of $2,000. Multiply that times the 5 years that these customers will stay with this business and a total value of $10,000 is generated from this $1,500 advertisement. The lifetime value of those 10 customers is $10,000, and that's not including any referrals they generate.

In determining the Lifetime Customer Value for your business, a good guide to start with is using 5 years for the duration of time a customer does business with you. However, to make the most accurate business and marketing decisions you need to figure out the exact number.

To give you an example of an industry that understands this concept, look at DVD and CD clubs. You have certainly seen their offers to order "5 Free DVDs for $1.00." Obviously it costs more than $1.00 to deliver 5 DVDs to your door.

These DVD and music clubs are savvy marketers that understand the concept of Customer Lifetime Value. They have calculated the average amount of time a customer continues to do business with them, and they know there will be additional orders that more than make up for the loss on the first order.

This lifetime value process is the same information used by manufacturers in determining whether to purchase a piece of equipment. They may not cover their costs up front, but over the lifetime of the equipment the return justifies their investment. You should think about marketing in the exact same way.

A shift in your thinking can give you incredible leverage in marketing your business. When you know your Lifetime Customer Value, you learn that you can actually spend more money to acquire customers. This gives you a great advantage over competitors in your marketplace because it allows you to think more strategically about growing your business.

Ultimately it comes down to two questions:

1. What **can** you afford to spend to attract new customers?
2. What are you **willing** to spend to attract new customers?

Depending on your strategic objectives, you may find that you can and are willing to spend four or five times more than your competitors spend. If your competitors don't keep up with you, they could lose a good portion of their business while you capture valuable market share.

CALCULATING THE LIFETIME CUSTOMER VALUE OF YOUR BUSINESS

The following is a breakdown of how to calculate the Lifetime Customer Value for your business:

1. The average purchase amount…
2. Multiplied by the average number of times a customer buys from you per year…
3. Multiplied by the average number of years your customers continue to do business with you.

Another computation you should make will give you the Lifetime Profit Value of a customer. This calculation figures the amount of profit each customer is worth to your business, but requires one additional step:

1. The average purchase amount…
2. Multiplied by the average number of times a customer buys from you per year…
3. Multiplied by the average number of years your customers continue to do business with you…
4. Minus costs, such as production, fulfillment, delivery, marketing, sales (commissions, salaries and bonuses), and any other overhead expenses.

Following is an example of the Customer Lifetime Value calculation for a restaurant:

	Customer Lifetime Value: Restaurant Example	
A.	Amount of average sale	$ 50
B.	Number of yearly purchases	20
C.	Yearly income per customer	$ 1,000
D.	Number of years customer patronizes restaurant	5
E.	Customer Lifetime Value	$ 5,000

F.	Overhead expenses:	$ 2,000
G.	Lifetime Profit Value of a Customer:	$ 3,000

As a business owner or executive, you need to find ways to increase the value you provide your customers so they will want to spend more money with you, more often, for a longer "buying lifetime", and send more referrals to your business.

THE COST OF LOSING A CUSTOMER

Along with understanding your Customer Lifetime Value, you must have a clear understanding of the real effects losing a customer has on your business.

One lost and unhappy customer can have a far-reaching impact on your business, because negative word-of-mouth travels faster and further than positive word-of-mouth. By understanding this concept, you realize that you're not only losing their business, but you lose the business of their potential referrals as well.

If an unhappy customer were to tell 10 people about their experience (or not refer those 10 people to do business with you), and each of those 10 people told 5 others, the total number of people affected by that one bad experience would be 61 (see calculations below).

If only 25% of those people chose not to do business with you because of this negative word-of-mouth, that totals 15.25 people.

If each of those 15.25 customers had buying habits like your original customer, the lifetime revenues lost can be astronomical.

Restaurant Example: Cost of Losing a Customer		
A.	The original unhappy "lost" customer	1
B.	Tells 10 others of their bad experience	10
C.	Who each tell 5 others	50

D.	Total people knowing of bad experience	61
E.	25% don't buy from negative word-of-mouth	15.25
F.	Lifetime Profit Value of a Customer	$ 3,000
G.	Total Lost Profits from one bad experience	$ 45,750

Expanding on the previous restaurant example, the preceding calculator illustrates the Cost of Losing a Customer: $45,750 lost from one bad experience!

Maybe you're having a hard time believing those figures, so let's cut those numbers in half... twice. You still have a total of $11,437.50 lost, and that's a lot of money for letting one person leave unhappy.

TO MAXIMIZE PROFITS YOU MUST HAVE A BACK-END

Regardless what business you are in, the difference between marginal profits and incredible profits lies in your back-end. Working and profiting from your back-end is easy... you just make regular and frequent offers that provide great value to your customer and client base. That's it.

If you deliver what you promise and establish strong trust and goodwill among your customers, you can leverage that relationship with them by offering them more value and benefits. Developing a strong back-end sales program can turn marginal advertising efforts into lucrative long-term relationships and profit centers.

Increasing your Customer Lifetime Value is directly related to how well you work and manage your back-end. Let me explain:

If you spend $2,000 to run an ad that brings you 40 new customers, and each one of them is worth $50 in profits to your business, then you have just broken even.

If you call those same 40 new customers a month later and sell 25% of them another product or service at $75 profit, your net profit is $750.

What if you can get five of those customers to enter into an annual contract with your business, guaranteeing you another 12 purchases during the year worth an additional $50 profit each? Now you have built an incredible and ongoing profit center that is worth an additional $3,000 over the next year.

That $2,000 ad that originally broke even was ultimately worth $5,750 to you because of the strength of your back-end.

A strong back-end allows you to commit as much money as you can to bring in new customers because your back-end profits will more than make up for any up-front losses. The easiest, most cost-effective sales to make are repeat sales to satisfied customers. Once you have an established customer base, your marketing costs diminish significantly.

Along with a successful back-end, you obviously want to have ads that generate profits on their own. The important point to understand is that ads that break even or lose a little money can be profitable when you are filling your pipeline with customers and clients who become profitable later in their lifecycle because of back-end business.

Remember the CD and DVD club example from earlier in this chapter? This is what makes their offers work so well. They sell 5 DVDs for $1 to bring in new customers, then they make all of their profits on the back-end.

Lead generation and conversion are the most expensive marketing processes for just about every business. Selling to your existing customers is much easier and more lucrative. By no means am I suggesting that you should stop trying to get as many new customers as you can. Remember, the real money is made by developing your back-end potential.

You wouldn't believe how many businesses never attempt to resell their customers... not even once! This is costing them a fortune and they don't even know it.

Since the real money is in back-end, don't let your back-end marketing campaign end with just one or two follow-up offers. The truth is that most businesses can make offers to their current customers once per month and still get incredible results. I know companies who consistently get 25% of their entire customer base to purchase something new from them every month. If you are an American Express member, or you have ever ordered from one of the big catalog companies, then you know what I mean. These companies know how to work their back-end.

Businesses that sell only one product or service sometimes have problems constructing back-end offers. If this describes your business, look for opportunities to license or sell the products and services of others. Develop joint ventures with owners of businesses offering complimentary products and services.

Remember, your customers trust you and are loyal to you. They would rather take your recommendation than gamble with a company they know nothing about. Your relationship with your customer has value, and that value is called "customer equity." Take advantage of your customer equity by continually making offers to your current and past customers.

Chapter 6:

Answering the Most Important Question in Business

Being unique to your prospects and customers in an advantageous way is the single most important key to achieving incredible business growth. Once developed, you must find ways to communicate that uniqueness effectively and consistently to your market.

There is a question that goes through your prospect's mind before they choose to do business with you. This same question goes through each of your customer's minds before they return to buy from you again.

"Why should I do business with you over all of the other options available to me, including the option of doing nothing at all?"

One of the most important decisions you will ever make in business is to establish a powerful answer to this question.

Without a powerful answer you become like every other business who sells the same products and services that you do.

It doesn't matter what you offer, your customers can go just about anywhere to find the exact same (or very similar) products or services for the same price, and probably even less money than what you charge.

If you expect people to do business with you instead of your competitor, it is imperative that you have something to offer that your competition does not. Ideally you want that advantage to be something your competition can't offer.

This is what is known as your Unique Selling Proposition.

There are many names for this strategy, including Unique Selling Advantage and Unique Competitive Advantage, and it is linked with the marketing strategies of positioning and messaging. We're going to keep this simple and use the term Unique Selling Proposition, or USP, because that is what ad man Rosser Reeves first wrote about in the 50's and 60's.

Your USP is what makes you unique from all your competitors, both locally and industry wide. Today's consumers have more choices available to them than at any other time in history. So now, more than ever before, you need to be different and able to give your market a valid reason to choose you over your competitors. Choosing to do business with you needs to be a "no-brainer."

The most successful businesses in an industry or profession aren't always the best, but they are almost always considered unique in some strong way. "Me too" businesses rarely survive and usually end up in price wars because they don't have anything unique to help them establish high value in the minds of their prospects. That leaves them with only one weapon to compete with, and that is price. Unless you have a significant cost advantage over all your other competitors, it is only a matter of time until you lose that competition.

A well thought-out and carefully defined USP is a strategic advantage that you need to have to maximize the growth of your business.

> "Differentiation is the cornerstone of successful marketing."
>
> **Philip Kotler**
> S.C. Johnson Distinguished Professor of Marketing
> Kellogg Graduate School of Management
> Northwestern University

Here's a simple test I would like you to perform that will be a good learning experience for you: Ask any 10 business owners, professionals, managers, entrepreneurs, or sales professional why you should do business with them and not their competition. You'll most likely hear the same answers over and over again. Answers such as, "We offer the highest quality products or services", "We offer the best customer service", or maybe "We have the lowest prices around."

Now ask yourself this question: What did you really learn from those kinds of answers? Does any of those answers really compel you to buy from them, or are they all "me-too", boring and forgetful statement that you've heard a million times before by countless other businesses?

If you are in business, or if you are responsible for attracting new customers to your business, then you need to have a ready, clear and compelling answer to the question of why someone should do business with you and not your competition. If you don't have a great answer to that question, then I can promise you that your business is underperforming.

We live in the most competitive business environment in history. Competition is more intense than ever, products and services are so similar, and prices are so aggressive that businesses are failing at alarming rates. It has become almost impossible for any business in any industry or profession to maintain a competitive advantage for any length of time based on the products they offer or the prices they charge.

The simple truth is that if you can't give your prospects and customers a clear and compelling reason to buy from you, then you can never expect your business to be any better than any of your competitors. You will be just another "me too" business in the eyes of your customers and your market.

Creating and utilizing a powerful USP in your business is not a new concept, but most businesses, including your competitors, don't do it. You cannot afford to miss out on this incredible competitive advantage.

THE STRATEGY AND SKILL OF POSITIONING

Not being able to clearly differentiate your business from the many other competitors or options available to your market is the biggest and most common marketing failure I see in business… and it's the most detrimental.

The ability to articulate a strong USP is the single most important strategic advantage you will ever have, and I can't stress enough how important this is to you. How can you expect your clients or customers to choose you over other options if they can't see what makes you unique and beneficial to them?

There have been many outstanding businesses founded on a USP alone. The most famous example is Domino's Pizza. Tom Monahan made Domino's Pizza one of the most successful fast food businesses in the world with the strength of the USP "Fresh hot pizza delivered in 30 minutes or less – guaranteed." This USP guaranteeing delivery propelled Domino's Pizza from a start-up to a $4 billion company in just a few years.

Suppose Domino's Pizza would have had the USP of "The fastest pizza delivery in town." Do you think that would have produced the same results? Not even close. That statement means absolutely nothing. There is no way to measure it and there is no way to hold the company accountable. Empty promises are worthless and can actually harm your business because people see right through them.

There's one more point I would like to make about the Domino's Pizza USP: There are now many pizza restaurants who can deliver your pizza in 30 minutes. It is no longer unique, and as a result, Domino's no longer rules the pizza delivery category.

USP LEADS TO COMPETITIVE ADVANTAGES

Another successful company known for their powerful Unique Selling Proposition is FedEx. It may come as a surprise to you, but FedEx was not an instant success. Their original strategy was to compete against Emery Air by selling a better service at a cheaper price.

FedEx had three different delivery services that competed directly with Emery Air, and they offered a price advantage as their differentiator. The three delivery services were:

1. Priority 1: Overnight delivery
2. Priority 2: 2-day delivery

3. Priority 3: 3-day delivery

In FedEx's first two years of operation they lost $29 million dollars. They had to do something differently or they would fail, so they refocused their strategy by emphasizing Priority 1 overnight delivery.

They dropped Priority 2 all together. Priority 3 was re-named "standard air service", and they introduced a courier package that held 2 lbs. of documents.

They also made one of the best strategic moves in the history of business and created the USP of, "When it absolutely, positively has to be there overnight."

They were no longer focused on being less expensive than their competition. They repositioned themselves as being the most reliable form of overnight delivery, giving them a new USP and more effective competitive advantage in their marketplace.

Do you know what happened to Emery Air? Trying to keep up, they bought Purolator Courier for $313 million, but this didn't keep them from losing $100 million the year.

The once dominant market leader now had to reposition and refocus their company to stay alive. New management took Emery out of the letter and small package segment of the overnight delivery market. They began concentrating their resources on delivery of freight packages weighing over 70 lbs.

Their new USP made Emery Air profitable all over again, with their operating profits exceeding $77 million annually.

The USP is the most important part of any marketing plan. The USP becomes the central concept and foundation of all the marketing and sales efforts of a company, including identifying which target markets you should pursue.

> "A successful competitive strategy is one that leads to a sustainable competitive advantage."
>
> **Michael Porter**
> Professor, Harvard Business School
> leading authority on Competition and Strategy

As Michael Porter said, creating a sustainable competitive advantage is a key to a successful business strategy. A strong USP is critical to creating a marketing strategy and action plan that drives you toward maximum growth.

To drive home this point, I want to share a couple of other relevant quotes by two of the most successful business people in US history:

> "If you don't have a competitive advantage, don't compete."
>
> **Jack Welch**
> Former CEO of General Electric
>
> ---
>
> "The key to investing is not assessing how much an industry is going to affect society, or how much it will grow, but rather determining the competitive advantage of any given company and, above all, the durability of that advantage. The products or services that have wide, sustainable moats around them are the ones that deliver rewards to investors."
>
> **Warren Buffett**

The "Oracle of Omaha", and perhaps the most celebrated investor in US history makes it very clear: a sustainable competitive advantage equates to business wealth.

In an age of extreme competition and thousands of marketing messages competing for our attention every day, it's more important than ever to differentiate your business and create strong, compelling competitive advantages that are important to your target market.

Think about competition during a recession - the same number of businesses are competing for a diminishing number of prospects. The competitive landscape becomes tougher and choices for buyers get more difficult. To survive in a slow economy it is even more important to differentiate your business in the eyes of the marketplace.

PERCEPTION IS REALITY

As I mentioned before, the most successful businesses are not always the best at what they do, but they are almost always considered unique. Marketing is often a battle of perceptions, not products and services. The real driving force in the marketing world is not quality, but the perception of quality.

Think about the famous example of the "Cola Wars" of the 1980s and '90s. People drink the label, not the contents of the soft drink bottle.

- Coca-Cola spent $4 million on 200,000 taste tests that proved New Coke tastes better than Pepsi.
- Pepsi spent millions on taste tests that proved Pepsi tasted better than Original Coke.
- Royal Crown Cola did a million taste tests that proved RC Cola tastes better than Coke (57% to 43%) and better than Pepsi (53% to 47%).

INCORPORATING YOUR USP INTO YOUR BUSINESS

Identifying, developing and incorporating your USP into everything you do can be challenging, but the reward is worth the effort. Remember, "me too" businesses rarely survive. They usually end up in price wars because they don't have anything unique about them to establish value in the minds of their prospects. Their only competitive weapon is price.

The USP forces you to be clear and precisely define the advantages your customers can expect from doing business with you. A clear statement of your USP is paramount to your success in marketing and maximizing business growth. It will become the cornerstone of your business, driving every aspect of your marketing and sales efforts.

> "The road to everything you desire is through your USP. You can make a lot of money without knowing your USP, but for every dollar you earn, you're probably leaving 10 on the table."
>
> **John Carlton**
> Word-Famous Direct Response Copywriter

According to Robert C. Smith of Jungle Marketing, Inc., a USP must accomplish several primary objectives:

- Attract attention
- Distinguish you from your competitors
- Motivate someone to take action
- Fulfill an industry gap

Your USP is that single, unique benefit or big promise that you offer to your prospects and customers – one that no other competitor offers, and one that motivates prospects to take action.

EXAMPLES OF GREAT USPS

Before you get started creating your own Unique Selling Proposition, let me give you several great examples of effective USPs that you're probably familiar with.

- Domino's Pizza: "Fresh, hot pizza delivered to you in 30 minutes or less – guaranteed."
- FedEx: "When it absolutely, positively has to be there overnight."
- M&Ms: "Melts in your mouth, not in your hands."
- LensCrafters: "Helping people see better one hour at a time."
- Roto-Rooter: "Call Roto-Rooter – that's the name – and away go troubles down the drain."
- Avis Car Rental: "We're number two. We try harder."
- L'Oreal: "The most expensive hair color in the world. Because I'm worth it."
- Kellogg's Raisin Bran: "Two scoops of raisins in every box."
- Anacin: "The pain reliever doctors recommend most."
- Rolaids: "How do you spell relief: R-O-L-A-I-D-S."
- Geico: "15 minutes could save you 15% or more on car insurance."

What do these slogans have in common? They are powerful statements that clearly position those businesses as being different from their competition. If a buyer wanted the benefits they promise, there is only one company that can provide them. This is a strategy you need to incorporate into your business.

Your goal with your USP is to lead your customers and prospects to the conclusion that your business is not only the logical consideration, but the only consideration for them. You want them to think, "I would have to be an absolute fool to even consider doing business with anyone else."

Coming up with your USP doesn't have to be difficult, but it is important to remember that is has to be perceived as valuable to your target market and customers. It's not what you think that counts, it's what your prospects and customers consider valuable that matters. They are the ones with the money; it is their vote that counts.

CREATING YOUR USP

Rushing or hurrying your USP is a mistake. Over the course of your business you will spend thousands to millions of dollars on advertising and promoting your USP, so you want to get it right. Having to change your USP in the future will not only cost you more money, but this type of strategic repositioning could confuse your customers and prospects.

To get you started on identifying and creating your USP, here are a few questions to ask yourself:

- Who is your target market?
- What are the most important results they want from the purchase of your product or service?
- What are three reasons why your best customers do business with you over your competition?
- What are the main problems of your target market as they relate to your product or service?
- How do you uniquely solve their problems?

If you are unclear about what your USP may be, listen to the top salesperson in your company. It is often instinctive for them to sell what the customers really want.

Now review the answers to those questions, highlighting the words and phrases that have the most impact in describing your products and services. Add any other thoughts or language that you think is important about your business and business goals.

Eliminate all the dead weight and whittle down the information you have to one pithy sentence (two at most) that incorporates all of your major points.

Take a break, then come back and polish it up until it is a clear, concise statement that has impact and salesmanship in every word. It doesn't have to "read well", but it does have to create tension, desire and urgency in the reader's mind.

INTEGRATE YOUR USP INTO EVERYTHING YOU DO

Sometimes a company can uncover or create a great USP but fail to integrate it successfully into their marketing efforts. Business leaders must require teams and departments to make the USP an integral part of their sales and marketing processes.

Your USP should be found in your advertisements, marketing communications, business cards, sales scripts, sales presentations, headlines, body copy of ads, direct mail, and all ongoing communications with customers. You can't overdo or wear out your USP, especially if it is powerful.

When evaluating marketing strategies and tactics in the future, if you find they do not align with your USP, just forget about them. There are other, more productive and effective activities you can focus your efforts on.

A FINAL THOUGHT ON THE USP

I can't stress enough how important the concept of creating and integrating a powerful Unique Selling Proposition is to your business success. **The lack of commitment to create and implement a strong USP is the single most common reason why I see otherwise good marketing fail.**

Dismiss this critical concept at your own peril.

Chapter 7:

Lead Generation

If you ask any business owner what would be required to take their businesses to the next level, almost all of them will answer, "More customers."

Getting new customers begins with finding someone to tell your sales story to – a prospect or a lead – and this process is called lead generation.

Simply stated, lead generation is finding ways to get in front of qualified prospects to tell your sales story to. There are literally hundreds of lead generation tactics and tools you can employ in your business, from direct mail, to paid advertising, free publicity, and joint ventures, to having your sales team make prospecting or cold calls.

Lead generation is the first growth key of the TriFecta Exponential Growth Model, and also serves as a growth multiplier. When all other growth factors remain, an improvement in lead generation of 10% will produce overall growth of your business by 10%.

Lead generation is the single area that most business owners, including your competitors, focus most of their time, efforts, and marketing dollars. If you've been in business for a while you probably realize that lead generation is not always the easiest or most profitable thing you can do, and it is almost always the most expensive type of marketing.

Every business or professional practice needs new customers and clients, but few really understand what has to happen to get new customers to purchase from them. There are several marketing functions involved in producing new customers, and include lead generation, prospect education, prospect conversion, and generating referrals.

Almost all businesses have each one of those functions in their process of increasing their number of customers, and all are very important. However, for many small and mid-sized businesses, lead generation is the only purpose of their marketing.

THE PROBLEM WITH MOST LEAD GENERATION PROGRAMS

Looking at lead generation a little more closely, you will find that most businesses have only one or two methods of attracting new prospects. It may be cold calling, running media advertisements, or it could be referrals. I want you to understand something: There's a huge flaw in operating your business this way. When you are dependent on one source for generating leads for your business, you are at risk of falling victim to any number of serious, business crippling problems.

First of all, media advertising can dry up. You may find that you no longer get the results you once did; results that your business has come to depend upon. There are many reasons for this, and if you've ever advertised consistently, you probably know what I'm talking about.

The second problem is that market dynamics can change. This could occur when a new competitor enters your market and they have a perceived advantage over you in the market place. There is also the fear of economic recession which can keep many customers from opening their wallets.

A third problem is depending on your sales people for all of your lead generation. Some sales people just are not very effective, especially at cold calling, and they are subject to any number of issues that range from turnover to personal problems. If you lost your number one sales person who generated a great portion of the leads for your company, it would have a devastating effect on your business.

What about your business? Chances are that you, just like almost every other business, utilize just one or two main methods of attracting prospects. Very likely the method you use is the same method almost every other business in your industry or profession uses. It's called the "that's how things are done in our industry" method.

Think about how the average business is started...

When a person first decides that they want to go into business, they typically have some industry experience, or they look around and see what everyone else in their industry is doing. Then they do what everyone else is doing to market or promote their business. This is how nearly every business in every industry or profession does their marketing.

There are two important things you need to understand about this method of marketing:

- Who set up that system in the first place? Who says it is right, or that it is the best system for you to use? The fact is there are an unlimited number of ways to attract new customers to your business, and your imagination is the only limiting factor.

- You will never become exceptional doing the same things as everyone else. You will be another "me too" company struggling to differentiate your business in the marketplace.

What about you? What marketing tools are you using to generate leads for your business? How many different marketing methods do you presently have working for you? There's a real danger in having only one of two main methods of attracting new customers. You are leaving yourself open and vulnerable to economic and competitive forces if you do. New leads are vital to the growth and survival of your business, and it's critical for you to have multiple systems in place generating new customers to ensure that your business keeps running and growing, uninterrupted if anything unexpected happens.

THE LEAD GENERATION MACHINE

Every business wants to generate more high quality leads, but very few do it well. I want to introduce you to the most powerful lead generation system I've ever experienced. I call it the Lead Generation Machine, or LGM for short, and I've used it successfully in dozens of different industries and business categories.

BENEFITS OF THE LEAD GENERATION MACHINE SYSTEM

The reason I call this system the Lead Generation Machine is because it contains all the components and qualities that a machine or system should have, such as...

- Requires little effort to run it effectively. In fact, you can practically put it on "autopilot."
- Generates names, addresses, and even email addresses of people interested in knowing more about the products and services you provide.
- Gives you permission to contact them and give them your best sales presentation about your product or service.
- Creates a relationship based on trust, showing your prospects that you are an authority in your industry about the products and services you provide.
- Generates predictable results. Because it's a system, you can make the machine run faster or slower when needed. It gives you control.

HOW THE LEAD GENERATION MACHINE WORKS

There are five steps in developing your LGM. Each step is important, so make sure that you take the time to do each step right.

Step 1: **List the top three reasons why your customers buy your product or service.** Why do your customers buy from you? Ask your sales people and your customers. You need to really understand the problems your customers are trying to solve when they buy from you.

Step 2: **Create a Lead Generation Magnet.** This "magnet" is in the form of a special report, and it should provide valuable "insider" information that the average prospects do not know about. It must be highly educational and not contain "sales" information. Your special report can be a written report, and audio CD-ROM, or a DVD video. Choose an exciting title for the report focused on the benefits your customers receive from you products and services. From my experience, some of the best titles start with "How To", use numbers, and are framed to avoid the fear of loss. For instance, "How to Avoid Six Common Income Tax Mistakes That are Costing You Thousands of Dollars."

Step 3: Develop a Direct Response Advertisement. Create a small ad that looks like a newspaper article and includes the following elements:

- A strong and compelling headline. Very often you can use the same headline as the title of your special report.
- Identify the main problem in the first sentence. For example: "85% of Los Angeles business owners are losing thousands of dollars every year by making dumb income tax mistakes."
- Announce your special report as the solution to their problem. You could write something like this, "Recently a new special report was released identifying what these income tax mistakes are and gives you a step-by-step explanation of how to avoid them."
- Tell people how to get the report and what benefits they will receive by acting immediately. For example, "Stop making these mistakes and save thousands of dollars in unnecessary tax payments by calling (555) 555-5555 and requesting your special report."

If you offer your report for free, you will increase the number of leads you generate, but some of those leads will probably be "tire kickers."

If you want to avoid this, you must make it a little more difficult for your prospects to respond. Charging a small fee for your free report (for postage and handling) will eliminate some of the "tire kickers", but you will probably want to deal with a few of them then lose some potential customers and clients.

Step 4: Set Up Your Response Mechanism. To make the most out of the leads you get, develop a response mechanism that logs all leads and tracks where they came from. How terrible of a mistake it would be for you to create a great special report, run a great ad, but then lose your valuable leads.

You can use a toll-free, direct response phone system to capture names and addresses. The phone makes it easy for prospects to respond, and using a toll-free number lowers the risk for the prospect. It also allows you to handle many incoming calls simultaneously without any effort on your part. I recommend using Automated Marketing Solutions (www.AutomatedMarketingSolutions.com) for your toll-free line. Their system was developed specifically for handling lead generation programs.

You will need to create a phone script welcoming the caller, repeating the offer, and inviting them to respond by leaving their name and address. You should also make a second offer for an extra free gift that you will email to them if they give you their email address.

Make certain to use the words "free recorded message" in your ad. This lets the prospect know that they won't be getting a sales pitch when they call, which will increase your response rate.

Step 5: Set Up a Follow-Up Fulfillment System. Suppose you run your advertisement and now calls are coming in requesting your free report. How are you going to manage all of your new prospects? Imagine that you are going to send them three to five follow-up marketing pieces – this could become a nightmare very quickly if you're not careful.

I highly recommend using a contact management system such as ACT or SalesForce.com to manage your leads. There are many other programs that can do the same thing, but these are the easiest to use. Both can keep your entire marketing program organized and easy to manage.

In ACT, you can set up an Activity Series to run a series of activities performed at specific times. For instance, if you just received a lead you will send out your special report immediately. You might call the prospect two days later, send a follow-up postcard five days after that, and finally send a sales letter with a great offer a week after that.

Once set up, the Activity Series attaches your new lead and the software does the rest. All you have to do is select the task list and it will tell you all the marketing activities you have to do that day for the prospects you are managing.

THE LEAD GENERATION MACHINE WORKS IN ANY MEDIUM

A common misconception people have is that you can't use the LGM on all media. That is not true. You can use any type of marketing medium to generate leads, including print media, radio, television, signage, trade shows, the Internet, joint ventures, etc.

One of the most impressive lead generation efforts I've ever implemented using the LGM was with a client that participated in a lot of trade shows. We created a large sign that said "Free Special Report! How to Save Thousands on Uniform Costs This Year." We posted a sign in the booth and had a sign-up sheet for people to leave their name and address, which we would use to send them the report.

The booth was half the size of the competitor's booths, but we ended up getting three or four times more leads as the larger competitors did. Better than that, my client was able to convert 20% of those leads to paying customers.

All of the most effective radio and television spots I have ever done offered a free report, CD, or DVD to the first 50 callers. I would never run a radio, television or print ad without offering a free report. Think about it, if you aren't able to get the name and address of the prospects generated from an ad, then it's an enormous waste of your advertising dollars.

WHY THE LEAD GENERATION MACHINE WORKS

Generating qualified prospects with the LGM is actually based on basic human psychology. People are motivated to take action by several simple psychological triggers:

- People are naturally curious and love to know information that other people don't know.
- People are turned off by traditional sales pitches. They want good, useful information that will benefit them as buyers. In fact, people are seven times more likely to read a traditional news oriented editorial style article than they are an advertisement.
- People pay attention to things that directly affect them. People suffering from arthritis will find information about arthritis interesting and read everything they can on the topic. Those who don't suffer from arthritis will not be interested in it at all.
- People are natural consumers. If you remove the risk from taking action, people are more likely to respond to your offer.
- People can't resist a free offer. Even though it's been done for years, the highest response rates come from free offers.

Combined together, each of these psychological triggers compels the average person to take action. Using these triggers in a powerful small business "advertorial advertisement" (a cross between an advertisement and editorial article) consistently brings in high quality leads.

MAKE THE LEAD GENERATION MACHINE WORK FOR YOUR BUSINESS

"This may work great for your business, but our market and customers are different. This type of lead generation won't work for us." I've heard this many times from business owners and clients, but time after time the system proves them wrong. The LGM works for just about any business that sells a product or a service.

If your business doors are open for any length of time, it's because you are solving some type of problem for your market. People exchange their money for your solution. All viable businesses solve some sort of problem.

What problems are you solving for your customers? You may be helping someone look or feel better, helping them save money, or making their lives easier in some way. The key to the LGM is offering special information that helps people avoid pain and achieve gain. If you do that, this system will work for your business. Just concentrate on what problems you solve and the rest will fall into place.

Put the Lead Generation Machine to work in your business right away. Not only will it improve your ability to generate quality leads, but it gives you more control over one of the most complex and important functions of business.

GETTING PROSPECTS TO CONTACT YOU

To maximize your overall effectiveness and efficiency, you cannot afford to be chasing down prospects trying to convince them to choose you or the products and services you offer. You must become proficient at getting qualified prospects to contact you wanting more information about what you do and how they can benefit from working with you.

When you contact someone with the intent of trying to sell them something (or even tell them about something you're selling), most of them couldn't care less. Very likely you interrupted what they were doing and are considered an uninvited pest to them.

When you call on a prospect, you are perceived as a "sales person." When prospects contact you, you are an advisor. That is why it is so important to have a lead generation system that entices prospects to contact you. Having them contact you is the only chance you have of breaking your prospect away from what they are doing and getting them interested in learning about the benefits of doing business with you.

EDUCATING YOUR PROSPECTS

You want to educate your prospects so well about what you offer and what you do that they'll not be able to resist contacting you. The LGM system establishes you as an expert and leader in your field. By sending them various forms of informational materials and tools such as special reports, audio CDs, videos, articles, newsletters, seminars, and workshops, you position yourself well above the other companies who consistently have their sales people hassling them without providing any real value.

DIRECT YOUR EFFORTS ON QUALIFIED PROSPECTS

When a prospect makes the effort to contact you via your LGM, they are identifying themselves as qualified prospects interested in the benefits that you provide. They give you their contact information in return for educational materials that will make them more aware and sophisticated buyers. They are literally asking you to follow up with them.

You no longer become the uninvited and unwelcome pest to them, and they are much more receptive to any calls or communications they receive from you.

Chapter 8:

Improving Conversion

Conversion is the process of turning prospects and leads into paying customers and clients. A customer is created when someone gives you money for the products and services you provide. Up until that point they are only prospects or shoppers.

If you are converting 20% of your prospects into customers, that means 80% of your sales and marketing efforts are failing. Every prospect that does not act as a result of your marketing efforts is costing you money in marketing costs, phone bills, salaries, and more. That is why it is so important to strive to achieve the highest conversion rate possible.

Selling efficiency rates can make or break a business. If you have never paid attention to your conversion rates before, start doing so now.

A Primary Key to Success in Business

Converting a higher percentage of prospects into paying customers is one of the essential components to success in your business, and it is the second growth key in the TriFecta Exponential Growth Model.

As with all of the Nine Growth Keys, our goal is to increase your conversion rate by 15% or better. That means you will generate 15% more customers from the same number of leads you are generating now.

Drastic measures are not required to improve your conversion rate by 15%. All you have to do is implement several of the tactics and tools covered in this chapter. I've seen cases where implementing just one of these tools has increased conversion by more than 50%, and many times have seen smaller improvements of 15-25%. You don't have to re-engineer your entire sales process, just add these tools to your current activities.

As you read through the following marketing tactics, find just one or two that will make a positive impact on improving your conversion, then put them to work for you. Take the tools that work and make them an ongoing system in your business. Sounds simple enough, doesn't it? Now let's get started.

HOW TO IMPROVE CONVERSION

You improve your conversion rate by getting better at what you do. This includes everything from your sales skills, sales process, and the marketing tools you use in your sales process. You can even focus your lead generation efforts to get higher quality prospects that are more likely to buy from you.

Improving conversion will require a bit of work and simple research. Through a three-stage process you will build a conversion system that constantly improves your sales efficiency.

Here are the three steps of improving conversion:

1. Focus only on highly qualified prospects
2. Build trust
3. Provide Proof

If you successfully do these three things you will have high conversion rates.

FOCUS ONLY ON HIGHLY QUALIFIED PROSPECTS

Not all buyers are created equally. Many companies waste time, energy and expensive sales and marketing resources on groups of people that aren't very likely to buy. That is why it's important to carefully select where you are going to spend your marketing budget, and on which groups of prospects.

Getting the right offer to the right market is the first step to improving your conversion rates.

- Do you know who your best prospects are?
- Do you know where to find them?
- Do you know the needs and wants they have?
- Do you know what kind of offers they respond to?
- What would prompt them to buy from you?
- What are their buying habits?
- Who do they associate themselves with?

If you don't know the answer to those critical questions, you will have a hard time improving your conversion rates. The more clearly you can focus on your target and niche markets, the more success you will have converting prospects into customers.

There's an incredible difference between a Suspect (just a name on a list) and a Prospect (someone who may be in the market for your product or service who also has the financial ability to buy). Don't waste your time, energy, or money trying to convince people who have no need, want, or capacity to buy from you.

SEGMENTING YOUR CUSTOMER LIST

Your customer and prospect list can be organized and manipulated in many different ways, such as by active customers, customers that spend the most money with you, recently inactive customers, and the types of purchases they made. It's one of the wonders of modern software. Ask your software provider for a program that will not only store your customer data, but allow you to easily and effortlessly examine the information from multiple angles at the stroke of a few keys.

Manipulating your customer data can help you find trends, spot buying patterns, and identify opportunities for more sales that you may not have thought of before. When it comes to making sales, knowledge is power, because this data can be used strategically for building your business.

BUILD TRUST

More than price, more than quality, and more than need, people buy from people they know, like and trust. If your market doesn't trust you, your business is in trouble. That's why it's important to establish trust right from the beginning.

Trust is based on several factors, with past performance being the most important. Other issues affecting trust are your willingness to stand behind and support your products and services, and your level of knowledge regarding your specialty and the market and industry as a whole.

GUARANTEES

For your customers, the benefit of your product or service is gained after the sale is made. Sometimes it can take days, weeks, months, and even years for them to realize these benefits. This makes the transaction with your company a risky one for the customer, and it is this risk that often prevents a customer from buying from you.

A prospect's resistance to buy is high because we're conditioned to be wary of marketing and sales hype. We all know that advertisers often stretch the truth about how a product or service will perform. Think about how many times you've been burned by some purchase. The experience sticks in your mind and creates skepticism, doesn't it?

You must overcome that natural resistance in your prospects. Creating ways to remove or reduce the risk of the transaction will make your prospects more inclined to buy from you and increase your conversion rates.

The primary way to eliminate this skepticism is to put the risk on yourself. This is called risk reversal, and it is simply removing barriers of entry away from the prospect and ensuring that they keep progressing toward the sale. The most common type of risk reversal is the guarantee, and the best type of guarantee is one that guarantees a specific result or benefit.

Depending on the product or service, offering a money-back guarantee can increase sales by 50% or more. Test your offer with and without a strong guarantee to see the difference.

A company that reverses risk and guarantees results gains an incredible competitive advantage in their marketplace, and they will be rewarded with more business. In fact, a risk reversal policy can be a very strong Unique Selling Proposition (USP) in itself. Entire businesses (very successful ones) have been built around the USP of risk reversal.

Remember learning about the USP in Chapter Six? Domino's Pizza guaranteed delivery in 30 minutes or less, and that USP guaranteeing fast delivery propelled them to the top of their industry in just a few short years.

Many business people don't like the thought of a "no questions asked" or "better than money back" guarantee. They worry they will be taken advantage of by unscrupulous buyers.

One of the keys to successful risk reversal is to offer a great product or service. When you do, the return and refunds will be minimal. Yes, there will be the occasional customer that will abuse your offer, but the increased sales you gain from risk reversal will greatly outweigh any returns. If you are failing to use a risk reversal strategy in your business, then you're not getting all the business you could.

A very powerful type of guarantee is the "better than money back" guarantee. It works by not only offering the customer their money back, but by also letting them keep any premiums or bonuses that were offered with the product or service.

It's important to know how well your guarantee is working for you before you make it a permanent part of your business. You can start by advertising your guarantee in a single marketing medium or allowing a couple of your sales reps to test it on 10 or 20 customers.

How much have sales increased because of the guarantee? Be sure to test at least two combinations of the guarantee to find the one that works best for you. You can offer a 30-day guarantee in one test and a 90-day guarantee in another. You may even want to test a lifetime guarantee.

Not only is a strong guarantee great at increasing conversion ratios, but it is also great at building repeat business. Your prospects and customers know you are an honest business and stand by your products and services. That kind of reputation spreads fast and translates into lots of positive word-of-mouth advertising, and that results in more new customer referrals.

BE THE EXPERT

It is impossible to build trust when you don't know your business. Buyers today are better educated than ever before, so you must know a lot more than the prospect to gain trust as an expert.

Whenever you cannot immediately answer a question a prospect asks, you lose an opportunity to impress… and to sell. Having a thorough knowledge of your products and services also aids in your ability to demonstrate effectively… and sell.

When you are comfortable in your expertise you can relax and show real passion about your products and services… and sell.

Positioning yourself as an expert requires doing something that makes you stand out as an expert. This could be:

- Writing a book.
- Publishing a regular newsletter or newspaper column.
- Giving seminars, workshops, and public talks.
- Getting invited on TV and radio talk shows.

- Issuing news releases related to the latest developments in your field and listing yourself as a resource for further information.
- Letting editors and reporters know that they can call you when they need information for a story that involves your expertise. They will then quote you and get your name in the news story and that is among the best kind of free publicity you can get.

Understand that you don't have to be a doctor, lawyer or other type of professional to be an expert. I know car mechanics, general contractors and landscapers that effectively use this tactic to drive new customers to their business.

EDUCATION

Why should your prospect pay the amount of money you are asking for your products or services? How good is it? What makes it so good? What makes it an offer of value? Why does it cost more or less than your competitor? Why is your offering better than your competitor's offering?

These are just some of the questions running through your prospect's mind when they consider making a purchase from you. If your product is cheaper than your competitor's product, does that mean it is of lower quality? What if your product is higher priced than your competitor's product, but they seem very similar... Why should your prospect pay more for yours?

This is an opportunity for you to build trust with that prospect. When you do everything you can to clear up any questions, you also clear away the prospect's resistance to buy, allowing them to make a fast and informed decision.

If you want to build trust with your customers, you should strive to educate them about your products and services. Tell them about the efforts that go into making your products, or the skills it takes to deliver your service. How much time does it take? How much value is delivered? Tell them about the features and benefits, with a focus on what those benefits will mean to your prospect.

Educating your prospects and customers adds dimension to your marketing message and value to your offering.

TRY BEFORE YOU BUY

With this tactic you allow a prospect to use a product before they pay for it, or keep it for free with the option of returning it within 30 days if they don't like it. The idea is that once they get used to having the product, they will want to keep it, and it can greatly increase the number of people who accept your offer.

Magazine and newsletter sellers live on this technique, but it can work well for others, too. Obviously it does carry some risk in that people may return the item, but it's an aggressive way to market and often pays off very well.

There are a couple of important points to making this tactic work. First, you need to have a highly qualified prospect. Second, you must provide a great up-front education or demonstration on how the product works and the benefits it provides. Third, you have to know your metrics and keep careful track of success and return rates.

This is a marketing tactic that you definitely want to test on a small scale.

PROVIDE PROOF

Selling isn't easy. Unless you can convince your prospect that your product or service will give them the result they need, you won't get the sale. Worse than that, people are more skeptical today than ever, so what you say to your prospects is often not believed or internalized.

How can you demonstrate to your prospects that you can deliver on your promises? It's actually easier than most people think: offer proof.

TESTIMONIALS

Testimonials are one of the most powerful tools marketers can use, but it is also one of the most underutilized. All of your sales and marketing materials, from media advertisements to sales pitches, should contain testimonials.

There are only three reasons why people don't buy from you:

1. They don't need your product or service.
2. They can't afford your product or service.
3. You haven't developed the trust or believability they need to feel comfortable doing business with you.

There's not much you can do about the first two factors, but there is a lot you can do to decrease their skepticism and establish the trust needed to accept your offer.

Using testimonials is one of the most effective ways to eliminate fear, increase the believability and credibility of your offer, and increase the number of leads generated from your promotions. In the eyes of your prospects, a testimonial is the most believable part of your advertisement or sales presentation. This is because the message is not coming from the seller; it's coming from an independent third party.

Prospects believe that a business will say just about anything to make a sale, and they are on constant lookout for deception. A testimonial from a "real person" is different. When a potential buyer reads or sees a testimonial from a third party, it becomes much more believable.

The best testimonials come from people who are in the same demographic group as your potential buyers. This makes the testimonial endorsement appear to be coming from a known and trusted person. Testimonials made by well-known or admired people (celebrities) are also very powerful tools of persuasion.

Testimonials don't have to be difficult to collect. One of the most effective ways to get them is to send your customers a questionnaire or evaluation form asking for their feedback on how they have benefited from using your product or service. The questions should be "open-ended" and ask for them to write down their feelings about their experience with your company and your products and services.

When you get positive feedback, have your customers sign a release statement giving you permission to use their testimony in your marketing. If you can include a picture or live video of satisfied customers giving their testimonial, that's even better. Also, use both the first and last name in your testimonials. A testimonial signed "J. Smith, New York" seems made up.

No marketing vehicle is complete without testimonials, so start collecting and putting them to use for your business today.

OTHER TYPES OF PROOF

If you are not using proof, you are making your sales and marketing processes much more difficult than necessary. Along with testimonials, consider adding some of these other tools to prove to your prospects that you deliver what you promise:

- Success stories and case studies.

- Pictures and video.
- Customer and client lists.
- Statistical proof.
- Physical demonstrations.

With proof, quantity and quality are both important. The point to remember is that you should include as much proof as you possibly can into your sales and marketing processes.

Simple tools like these can have a tremendous impact on your conversion rates, so start adding proof to all your sales and marketing efforts right away.

ADD LEVERAGE TO YOUR SELLING EFFORTS

There are many things you can do to make selling easier and more effective, and the more tools you have working for you, the more sales your business will make. The following selling "tools" can all make an immediate positive impact on how well you convert prospects into customers.

YOUR UNIQUE SELLING PROPOSITION

One of the most important factors in increasing closing ratios is to be "unique" from all the other competitors and options your market has when searching for the products and services you offer. Your USP enables you to stand out in a crowded marketplace, and it's the single most important strategic initiative of your marketing program.

DEMONSTRATIONS

A thorough, engaging and entertaining demonstration of your product or service is another powerful selling tool.

If you've ever watched the home shopping channels or an infomercial featuring Billy Mays, you know that demonstrating is a highly developed art. Watch the pros, read up on proper sales demonstration techniques... you don't want to just "wing it" when it comes to using this marketing tool.

Getting customers involved in the demonstration is a very effective marketing tactic. With this type of sampling, the customer gets to experience your product or service and "takes ownership", even if it's just temporary.

Demonstrations can be done live and in-person, or you can demonstrate over television or video. If you decide to demonstrate via video, consider hiring a professional to produce the video for you.

FOLLOW-UP

Following up with prospective customers is one of the most cost-effective and profitable activities you can do to build your business. It doesn't have to be an elaborate system or plan, and it doesn't have to be costly. However, your follow-up strategy needs to be well thought out and tailored to the unique wants of your prospects and customers if you want it to be successful.

Rookies take the first rejection as the last. Experienced sales professionals know that the vast majority of sales are not made on the first prospect contact. These prospects are usually closed on the third, fourth, fifth contact, or more. Relatively few customers will say "yes" today, but many more will say "yes" in the future.

One of the secrets to effective follow-up is to do it in different ways. Don't just bombard your prospect with phone calls. Send them letters, newsletters, special reports and articles to add variety to your communications between your phone calls.

Effective follow up after an initial contact can be one of the most powerful tools in your marketing arsenal for closing a higher percentage of prospects.

PREMIUMS

Including a "bonus" to give what you are selling greater value is a powerful way to make more sales, get higher prices, and make your customers and clients better satisfied all at the same time.

The challenge is to find a product, service, or something else that can be added to your offer that makes the customer think they are getting a great deal. People can't resist the lure of getting something for free, and as "worn out" as it may seem, it is still a powerful tool for increasing conversion rates.

The best premiums are low-cost, but have high perceived value to the person you're making the offer to. A great example of this is free educational information such as books and special reports as free giveaways for new customer lead generation activities.

The special report could be a written document, audio CD, or a DVD video containing material your prospects and customers will be interested in knowing. Videos have an especially high perceived value, and here are a few I have seen work very well:

Sporting Goods Retailer

- "Advanced Trolling Techniques for Saltwater Fish"
- "Successful Fly Fishing Strategies"

Salon

- "40 and Over Makeup Techniques"
- "Hollywood Makeup Secrets"

Car Dealership

- "Guide to Buying Your Next New Car"
- "The Smart Consumer's Guide to Buying a Used Car"

Using premiums is an effective marketing tactic when used correctly. Think about what you can offer free-of-charge that your prospects will consider valuable, and that is low cost to you. Don't forget to compute your Customer Lifetime Value so you know how much you can afford to invest to attract new customers.

DOWN-SELLING

If your customer is not taking you up on your offer for product "A", down-sell them to your lower priced model "B." You always want to sell your highest profit item first, but if it's clear that your prospect isn't going to purchase the more expensive product or service, offer them a lower price alternative.

Often when customers are hesitant, it could be the price they are concerned with. When you are prepared with a down-sell sales pitch and product/service, often times this will help you close the deal, and that is much better than losing the sale.

MAKE AN OFFER

If you think about it, all business can be boiled down to one thing: Make an offer. One entity offers another entity something in return for something else. Author Mark Joyner calls it "the core imperative of business."

With this in mind, it's amazing how many sellers never even make an offer. Listing your price, defining quality and benefits, providing testimonials, and a giving a great demonstration are wonderful, but you still need to make an offer. An offer says: "If you buy, here's what I'm prepared to give you or do for you in return."

"Buy one, get one free" is an offer. "Money-back guarantee, no questions asked" is an offer. Selling at 50% off is an offer to sell at half price. An offer is something that grabs a prospect and makes them think, "Hey, I'm being offered this, and I want it!"

In sales training you are taught to always ask for the order. Why do we not do it in our marketing?

How clear is your offer? What does your offer include? If you don't know, well, then you have a problem. Make an offer part of every marketing activity.

LIMITED TIME OFFERS

What type of offer do you think will pull the greatest response: A great deal on a product or service, or a great deal on a product or service that can only be taken advantage of in the next 48 hours?

By putting a limit on an offer you create a sense of urgency, and this will always improve your conversion. Because it works so well, the limited time offer is a tactic that is used by sellers everywhere and in every industry.

Tip: Give your customers a legitimate reason for the limited time offer (prices are increasing, limited supply, etc.), and stick to the time limitations you state. If you don't, it could cause you real problems later.

AN IRRESISTIBLE OFFER

Making an offer is important, but not all offers are created equal. The fact is that there are many other businesses out there that provide the same products and services as you. To increase your conversion rate, you need to craft your offer in a way that stands out from the rest.

There are many things you can do to make your offer unique. Since the offer is the "core imperative of business", it should be strategically structured in a way that makes it nearly impossible to compare with those of your competitors. When you present your offer to a highly targeted group of your prospects, it should be nearly impossible to say no to.

Here are a few tips on creating offers that are hard to resist:

- Add bonuses
- Limit supply
- Discounts
- Extended warranty
- Free consultation or service
- Free trial offers
- Back-end offers
- Loss leader offers
- Early-bird discount
- Preferred customer offer
- Buy one, get one free (or at a discount)
- Match or beat the best price
- Returned merchandise offer
- Special price for beta testers
- Rebate offer
- Damaged product sales
- Special price in return for feedback
- Trade-in offer
- Money-back guarantee
- Better-than-money-back guarantee
- The cheap alternative offer
- The deluxe alternative offer

- Mystery bonus offer
- Future bonus offer
- Free bonus for telling your friends
- Payment plans
- Free trial
- One-time offer
- Bundling or package deal offer
- Promise a specific result
- Reverse the risk
- Promise a high return on investment
- Special sale or discount

Chapter 9:

Referrals

Generating more referrals is the third growth key for increasing the number of customers that patronize your business.

For the small business, referral marketing is one of the most important and effective techniques for creating new prospects and clients. Anyone who has been in business any length of time has learned to appreciate referrals for several reasons:

- Referral customers are typically more profitable and loyal than customers coming from other sources.
- With referral customers, you rarely have to compete on price and the closing process is usually much faster and more efficient.
- Referral customers tend to be ones you enjoy working with and often refer even more business to you.

With referral marketing being such a powerful business building tool, it is a shame that less than 10% of all businesses have a formalized system to produce referrals. Without a formal process and system to generate referrals, businesses don't come close to reaching their referral potential.

The good news is that **most businesses can easily double the number of customers and clients they receive from referrals**, and they can do it very easily.

If you have a good product or service, then you should receive referrals or recommendations from your clients and customers. The better you are, the more unsolicited referrals you should get.

However, if you want to get many times more referrals than you are currently getting, then you need to create a proactive referral process and system. This is something that very few businesses do, and it is causing them to miss out on many of their ideal customers.

WHY REFERRALS ARE SO IMPORTANT

Think about this: **If you got just one referral from 50% of your clients or customers every year, what difference would that make to your business?** You would grow your customer base by 50% every year, and your business would double in less than two years.

Referrals are powerful because they come from credible third-party sources that have already experienced the benefit of doing business with you. When they come from a trusted friend or professional colleague, they're even more powerful because you know that person doesn't have an ulterior motive for providing the referral.

According to the Word-of-Mouth Marketing Association, 76% of buyers don't' believe your ads. Don't take it personally; they believe businesses will say anything in their advertising to generate response, even if it's untrue.

However, 68% of consumer and business-to-business buyers trust recommendations from their peers. This makes word-of-mouth marketing the most effective type of marketing because it is the most believable.

There is another powerful reason why you should create proactive referral programs in your business, and that is because customers that give referrals become more loyal to you and your business. When they recommend you to their friends and colleagues, psychologically they are becoming more attached to your business through the endorsement.

EARNING THE RIGHT TO REFERRALS

The majority of business leaders and entrepreneurs have two common misconceptions about referrals:

First, they believe they get far more referrals than they really do. Second, they believe great customer service will result in referrals. Although great customer service is critical to the success of your referral program, it doesn't guarantee you will get referrals. Receiving a large number of referrals on an ongoing basis is most often a result of deliberate planning.

You need to have a well-planned and proactive effort to generate referrals. Not only does your effort need to show your customers how to give referrals, but it should also recognize them for their efforts.

There are basically three types of customers:

1. Satisfied Customers have received exactly what they were expecting when they paid for your product or service.

2. Unsatisfied Customers feel they have somehow been shortchanged. They received less than what they expected from the transaction.
3. Thrilled Customers have had their expectations exceeded. In their minds they received more than they expected and greater value than they paid for.

The value your customers receive from doing business with you may be real value, or it may be perceived value. In the context of receiving referrals, it doesn't matter if it is real or perceived. After all, what is perceived in their mind is real to them... whether it's reality or not.

For that reason you must continually increase and provide your customers with both real and perceived value. The more you provide, the stronger your relationships with your customers will be, the closer they will move toward "thrilled" status, and the more likely they will be to refer others to you.

How do you accomplish this? How do you create as many "thrilled" customers as possible that will want to refer business to you?

> Do what you do so well that they will want to see it again and bring their friends.
>
> **Walt Disney**

That quote from Walt Disney is the strategy he used for marketing Disneyland, and he said it could apply to any business, regardless of what it sold or offered.

You're not trying to meet your customer's expectations; you're trying to exceed them. Similar products and services can all be expected to perform similarly. When it comes to the attention, care and service we receive, we all have our perceptions of what "good" means.

THE DIFFERENCE BETWEEN WORD-OF-MOUTH AND REFERRALS

In my approach toward referral marketing, there is a clear distinction between word-of-mouth and referrals. Word-of-mouth is more accidental than it is planned. Word-of-mouth happens when a customer or friend mentions your business in a conversation. You can't depend on it as a steady source of new leads for your business.

Referrals are the result of a carefully planned strategy and system that you put into place to generate new prospects and customers through your relationships with other people and businesses. By definition, a referral "system" is a process that can be turned on or off and produces predictable results.

Your business needs word-of-mouth advertising, but you gain much more power and far greater results by creating and implementing referral systems in your business.

HOW TO INCREASE REFERRALS

There are dozens of different ways to increase the amount of referrals you receive. For the sake of simplicity, we are going to focus on two types of referral processes that you can put to work for your business to bring in new customers: passive and active referral systems.

All businesses get referrals. Happy customers tell others about your products and services and, in turn, you get referrals. This is word-of-mouth business is more a results of luck than it is a referral system.

In contrast, with a Passive Referral System your clients are aware of your referral program and the benefits they receive from referring their friends. Although you create a systematic process for asking for referrals, you do not direct the process.

With an Active Referral System, you direct the referral process and motivate your customers to tell others about you. And as a result, they become your most effective promoters.

THE PASSIVE REFERRAL SYSTEM

A passive referral system involves systematically asking satisfied customers for referrals and following up diligently on those leads. This is the basic starting point for your referral program. Most businesses can double the number of referrals they receive simply by putting a system in place to regularly ask their customers and clients for referrals.

The downside is that passive referrals systems are only effective if you have a follow up system in place. Depending on the type of business you're in, this can be an impersonal introduction to the prospective customer.

Getting customers and clients to call and tell two or three people about your product, service or business, will improve results tremendously. As you can imagine, this is completely different than calling a referral cold. If your customer calls first, you are in essence following up on a warm lead and the referred prospect is much more likely to listen to you.

An even better system would be to have your clients call and notify you if one of their friends or colleagues were interested in your products or services. You would then be following up on a hot lead.

Your Referral Prospects

Your referral prospects are the referrals your customers send to you. You must have a thorough system of explaining your competitive advantages, the specific benefits you provide, how they will be treated, and what incentives you will provide for the opportunity to serve them.

Providing incentives to your referral prospects is not required, but it can give you an incredible boost in response. If you have a unique product or service or an incredibly high client satisfaction rate, then it will be easier to generate referrals without an incentive.

Here are a couple of different types of incentives that you can use to motivate your prospects:

- **Free trials**. This is an incredibly powerful way to get new referral prospects to try your product or service. If your Lifetime Customer Value is significant, free trials can work very well for you. Free trials are easy to test on a small scale, so there is very little risk involved.
- **Bonus offers**. A bonus offer allows you to provide the referral prospect with high perceived value for little cost. The bonus should be related to your product or service.

Arming Your Customers

Now it is time to arm your prospects to be your promoters. To get quality referral leads that convert at high rates you will want to speak with them yourself.

Alternatively, you should provide your customers with written and other support materials which they can share with their friends, family, colleagues, etc., that will communicate the same message. For your customer this includes a brochure or a one or two page description of your products or services that details both the advantages you offer and the benefits derived from them.

Along with your company information you will also need to provide a single-page letter that tells them how your referral program works. This should include:

- How the referral will be treated.
- The incentives the referred prospect receives on behalf of the customer.
- The types of prospects you are looking for, so you don't get unqualified people taking advantage of your incentive or taking up your time.
- What's in it for the customer.

METHODS FOR OBTAINING REFERRALS

Getting a customer or client both willing and motivated to generate referral prospects is the tricky part, because it requires the client to take significant action. Making this method work for your business depends on both your business and your relationship with your customers and clients.

If you were to ask your customers whether they know anyone that may be interested in your products or services, you will get minimal results that are often very unqualified. Instead, you should ask more focused questions that trigger your customer's memory and pinpoint the viable prospects.

Here are five techniques for obtaining quality leads from referrals:

1. **Ask a leading question**. This technique helps you pinpoint exactly what type of referral you want. For example, "Do you know anyone with back or neck pain?" Or, "Do you know anyone who is unhappy with

their current hair style?" You can ask customers or clients about their satisfaction with your business. If they are happy, then ask if they know others that have similar problems and needs as themselves.

2. **Use a referral list**. This works well if you are targeting specific types of businesses. For example, an accountant specializing in working with medical professionals could ask what surgeons, general practitioners, chiropractors, dentists, etc., that his client knows, triggering the client to think of specific people.

3. **The Rolodex concept**. This is where you ask your client to use their Rolodex, phone or address book to identify five or 10 names that fit your criteria. Again, you must educate them on the type of business or person you seek to stimulate quality referrals.

4. **Who your clients know**. When your client isn't a good referral source, you can ask them to introduce you to other people that may be good referral sources.

5. **Sending periodic self-mailers**. This involves sending your clients a mailer, such as a postcard requesting a few referrals. Ideally your campaign should encompass several delivery methods. This could start with educating the customer at the point of sale about your referral program, then following up with a letter re-introducing the program and asking for referrals.

THE TIMING OF OBTAINING REFERRALS

Taking the time to educate customers and clients about your referral program is very important. It doesn't mean you should ask for referrals on every contact, but instead educate them on the benefits you provide, relating success stories of someone that was referred to you, and so on.

Here are five common opportunities to ask for referrals:

1. **Point of Purchase**. It's always best to catch the client at their peak level of satisfaction, as they will be most enthusiastic about providing referrals and testimonials. Once back in their busy lives they quickly forget how happy they were with you. And sometimes, something down the road reduces their enthusiasm.
2. **Within a few days after servicing the client**. If the point of sale is an inappropriate time to ask, you may consider sending a letter or postcard asking for referrals within a few days after delivering your product or service.
3. **After a certain number of transactions**. Some people will want to wait until there is an established relationship with a client before asking for referrals. Even if you wait until the fourth or fifth purchase when there is a greater level of trust, asking at the point of purchase is still the best timing.
4. **After you receive positive feedback from the client**. If these previous approaches make you uncomfortable you may wish to wait until you receive positive feedback from clients before asking for a referral. Again, the client is at a high level of satisfaction, so the timing is perfect.
5. **On a periodic basis**. Depending on the type of business, some find they can get new referrals from customers every 6-12 months. You will have to experiment with this one, but the point to remember is that you don't ask for referrals just once and assume there are no more referrals to get from the customer. Situations, relationships and needs are constantly changing, and a properly motivated client may want to give you additional referrals.

ACTIVE REFERRAL SYSTEMS

Active referral systems take referrals to the next level because you direct the referral efforts and motivate customers to become your promoters.

With passive referral systems, it is up to you to follow up on referral prospects. These prospects may be unaware of you and may not have a need for your products or services, often resulting in unqualified referral prospects.

Active referral systems ensure all of your satisfied clients are educated on both the benefits of using your products or services and the specifics of how the referral program works. As previously noted, this is accomplished by arming them with information and incentives.

As with a passive referral system, the first step in getting quality referrals involves educating customers on the products and services you offer, what benefits you provide them, how their referral prospects will be treated, and what is in it for them. Don't make the mistake of thinking that your customers already know everything you offer to satisfy their needs.

The next step is to explain to your customers how you will treat the people they refer to you. Active referrals come to you with high expectations that are created by your customer's endorsement. If you don't deliver what they expect, not only will you lose them as a customer, but you could damage your relationship with your referring customer. Even if you don't lose them as a customer, too, it's not very likely they will ever refer additional business to you again.

Finally, you should provide some sort of incentive to motivate your customers to give referrals. Here are five ways you can achieve this:

1. **A simple "thank you."** Send a "thank you" note whenever you get a new client that they referred. Although this is a nice gesture, a more compelling offer will produce much better results.

2. **A token of appreciation**. Referrals are a result of providing superior service and value to your clients, so some will refer you without any incentive at all. However, almost everyone appreciates a small gesture of gratitude after they have referred you.

3. **Make the customer a hero**. If you can get your clients to give incentives to their referrals, you will make them look good in the eyes of their friends and colleagues. An example would be giving your clients gift certificates or special coupons only for their referrals to use.

4. **A bonus offer**. You could offer clients a bonus for any referral they send, such as a free service or special discount.

5. **A jackpot offer**. After a client has given you several new referral customers, consider giving them a large, special reward in relation to what you sell. You want to do something really special for them to motivate them to continue sending more referrals.

CONCLUSION

Establishing both passive and active referral programs with your customers and clients is an incredible opportunity for most businesses, especially small ones. By systematizing these referral processes, you can take advantage of one of the greatest and most effective opportunities you have to grow in sales, profits and market share.

Chapter 10:

Customer Reactivation

Customer reactivation is the fourth and final growth key that falls under the growth category of increasing the number of customers of a business.

Every business that has been around for at least a couple of years has past customers who no longer purchase products or services from their business. These customers and clients become inactive for a variety of reasons, but whatever the reason, they are no longer doing business with you.

At one time these customers liked your business and trusted you enough to purchase from you. Maybe a certain sale or offer you ran brought them to you, or maybe you were conveniently located to them. Regardless of how you attracted them in the first place, at one time they did buy from you.

These are your "inactive" customers. They have done business with you in the past, but are no longer considered "active" because they have not purchased from you recently.

Here is something that's very important to understand: **Just because they haven't purchased from you recently, that doesn't mean they won't purchase from you again.**

These inactive customers represent incredible opportunities to increase your sales and profits. Past customers are almost always the easiest sales to make, and you can get them back into the habit of conducting business with you more quickly and inexpensively than finding new customers. You already know how to contact them, and the cost of making contact is minor compared to the cost of finding and creating a new customer.

With your past customers you have already overcome the most difficult challenge in marketing – getting the prospect to trust you enough to give you money. People are naturally skeptical of any new business. They've become accustomed to businesses over-promising and under-delivering; therefore they're reluctant to do business with people they don't know.

WHY CUSTOMERS BECOME INACTIVE

As I mentioned earlier, every established business has inactive customers. Nearly every business focuses their marketing efforts on obtaining new customers and sales, often forgetting about their existing and past customers.

One of the most common mistakes businesses make is that they fail to keep in touch and market to their current and past customers. If you provided them with good value and service they will remember, and it won't take much effort to get them to do business with you again.

But what if they don't think that you took care of them in the best way possible, or that you didn't provide them with exceptional value? It doesn't mean these customers are lost forever, and it doesn't mean they don't still represent a tremendous profit opportunity. You just need to know how to capitalize on this "inactive" business asset.

There are three general reasons people stop buying from you in the first place, provided they haven't died or moved away. People stop doing business with a company because:

1. They have outgrown the need for the product and service you sell. They stopped buying because their needs have changed.
2. They have had a bad experience with either a product or service they bought, or with a certain company policy or person they dealt with.
3. They got out of the "habit" of doing business with the company.

Even if you made a mistake or your former customer had a bad experience with your business, an apology or explanation of the circumstances may help rebuild the old relationship.

If these past customers left your business to go with a competitor, it's only a matter of time before they will have a negative experience with them. How many businesses, in any industry or profession, are at the top of their game at all times?

Regardless of the reason for your customer leaving you, the end result is the same. Considering how difficult and expensive it is to get a new customer in the first place, you owe it to your business to do everything possible to get them to come back.

When you are dealing with former customers you are appealing to people who have used your products or services in the past, and they still may need or benefit from them. It may only take a minimal effort to reactivate them.

Depending on the type of business you have and the products and services you offer, the revenues generated by reactivating your inactive customers can quickly flood your business with high profits at low customer acquisition costs.

HOW TO REACTIVATE YOUR INACTIVE CUSTOMERS

The first step in reactivating these inactive customers and clients is to identify who they are.

How often do your regular customers do business with you? How often do you think your customers should do business with you? Each industry and profession is different. An inactive customer for one business may mean the customer hasn't purchased in 90 days; for another business it could be a year. It's up to you to decide what works for your business based on the average purchase frequency of your customers.

Now that you have your list of inactive customers, you need to communicate with them. It's imperative that your message:

- Thanks your customer or client for having done business with you in the past.
- Reminds them of the benefits they received from your products and services.
- Takes responsibility for having "neglected" them, making it clear that if you did something wrong you will do everything you can to remedy the problem.
- Offers to make it up to them.
- Present a special, time-limited offer that your inactive customers will find difficult to pass up.

It is absolutely critical that you make them an offer.

Make the offer as good as you can. Remember, once they are an active customer again, you can work them back into your regular sales process and you will gain additional revenues from them. Even if the first sale doesn't generate profits, it gets them back into the habit of doing business with you, and that is your primary goal.

A common misconception that business leaders have about this process is that they are going to make their inactive customers and clients upset. You worry that if you send them a letter, they will just crumple it up and throw it in the trash; or they will hang up if you make a phone call to them.

Consider this: Even if they do hang up on you or throw your letter away, it doesn't matter. These customers were "dead" to you in the first place. You are not in danger of ruining a relationship with a dead customer.

CUSTOMER REACTIVATION – WHAT CAN YOU EXPECT?

Reactivating inactive customers can have an incredible effect on your business. Depending on your type of business, it's not uncommon to experience a reactivation success rate of 10-25%. The key is to make them an incredible offer designed to create immediate sales and that they will have a hard time refusing.

How often should you try to reactivate your inactive customers? That depends on your business model and industry. I know some businesses that successfully run reactivation programs every quarter, each time bringing 10-20% of their inactive customers back to them. An annual customer reactivation campaign is appropriate for most companies.

While the first time you run a customer reactivation program usually produces the greatest results, as long as you have a strong offer, you will get results each and every time.

Chapter 11:

Increasing the Size of Purchase

The next growth key falls under the growth category of Increasing Average Transaction Values, and it is to increase the size of purchase.

In the previous three chapters we discussed getting more new customers and clients for your business. While that is a very important function for all businesses, it is typically the most expensive and least effective way to increase your profits.

This chapter introduces you to perhaps the simplest way to increase profits with literally no effort, no investment, and no risk at all.

But first I would like to ask you a few questions…

Have you ever been through a McDonald's drive-through and heard the questions, "Would you like fries or a drink with that?" Or, "Would you like to super-size your order today?"

Did you know that McDonald's, one of the largest companies in the entire world, consistently produces 30% of their entire profits from asking this question and applying this marketing strategy?

Many businesses have extensive and expensive plans, programs and marketing activities designed to acquire new customers, but only a few pay much attention to the growth key of increasing the size of the order.

McDonald's spends close to a billion dollars annually on advertising worldwide, and their brand was valued at $25 billion in 2005 (Restaurants & Institutions, 2005). Even with such marketing firepower behind them, they still earn 30% of their profits from asking a simple question at the point of sale!

We can all learn something from McDonald's... and I mean all of us. The growth key of increasing the size of purchase is applicable to every business.

YOU OWE IT TO YOUR CUSTOMERS

You have an obligation to your customers and clients to ensure they get the best value and benefit from their transaction with you. If you have additional products and services that can enhance that value, then it is your obligation to do everything that is ethical and reasonable to see they at least have the option of taking advantage of those benefits.

Your customers are continually searching for ways to satisfy their needs. As long as your offer to them is focused on their best interest and on what they are trying to achieve, then you will maintain the trust you have built with them. The key is to provide value that exceeds the price they pay you, and if they like your offer, they will happily buy from you.

HOW TO INCREASE THE SIZE OF PURCHASE

THE UP-SELL

The first tactic you can use to increase the size of each purchase is up-selling. This tactic is very simple: when a customer or client buys something from you, just make them an offer for more expensive products or services. Your goal when creating up-sells is to add so much value that your offer becomes irresistible.

Technically, an up-sell is the process of persuading buyers to purchase a larger or premium version of the same product or service. Up-sells also include making an offer of a premium package of products and services.

Your goal when creating up-sells is to add so much value that your offer becomes irresistible. Value = Perceived Benefits ÷ Price. If the price were to stay the same, but the perceived benefit goes up, then value increases.

The up-selling process attempts to increase the perceived benefit more than the increased price. The result is an increase in value... and hopefully a successful up-sell.

Super-sizing your order for a soft drink or coffee is an example of an up-sell. Another example would be when an insurance sales agent lets their client know that if they purchase a slightly larger policy, they will qualify for a lower price per thousand dollars of coverage. Businesses in every industry and profession can and should offer similar upgrades.

OFFER YOUR CUSTOMERS A GREATER QUANTITY

An up-sell can be as simple as offering a better deal for the purchase of a greater quantity. This is what McDonald's is doing when they "super-size" your order.

With this up-sell, all you are doing is offering them more of what they are already buying, but at a minimal price difference. When people are in the buying mode they are highly susceptible to buying more. Why wouldn't your customer want to buy more of what they have already decided to buy, especially if they can do so at a nice discount?

OFFER COMPLEMENTARY PRODUCTS AND SERVICES

You can also up-sell additional products and services to the original order. The idea is to create higher priced "upgrades" that offer a discount off their regular price.

Once again, there is literally no effort or investment added other than the actual cost of the product or service you are providing. The difference in income you receive is nearly all profit, since there are no customer acquisition costs to deduct.

Positioned properly, you can achieve up-sell success rates of 30% or more, and I have seen this result in dozens of different business categories. On top of that, companies successfully implementing this marketing tactic can earn as much as 30-50% of their profits this way.

The fact is that most customers want to be up-sold. They want greater value for their money, and they want to feel like they got a great deal. Up-selling can help them feel better about conducting business with you as long as you are providing them with more of the benefits they want at a more advantageous price.

There are many different ways to up-sell your customers, clients and patients. The two primary factors in creating a successful up-selling program are to get the timing right, and to add value by offering greater benefit to the customer. Here are a few up-sell ideas to get you started in creating your own up-sell program:

- Volume discount
- Special package price
- Deluxe version
- Buy two, get one free
- Extended warranties
- Buy two, get free shipping
- Longer subscription or membership
- Buy one, get second at a discount
- Combination of products and service

THE CROSS-SELL OR ADD-ON

Cross-selling involves offering your customer an additional product or service that they did not originally intend to purchase, and it is another very effective way to increase the size of purchase. Just like the up-sell, other than the actual cost of the products and services involved, the additional sales you make will be almost all profit since there are no customer acquisition costs involved.

A cross-sell can be related or unrelated to the originally purchased item. When someone makes a purchase from you, they have decided that they trust you and your company to deliver the product or service they bought. Stay within that area of trust.

Ask yourself this question when choosing cross-sells: "Will making this cross-sell advance or improve the outcome the customer is trying to receive?" If you can answer that question with a "yes", then your cross-sells will work well.

PACKAGING OR BUNDLING

Packaging, bundling, or combining several items together and giving a discounted price is another way to get your customers to spend more money while getting greater value.

McDonald's does this by bundling a hamburger, fries and a drink together and offering you a "Happy Meal." The price for this package is less than if the customer were to purchase each of those items separately.

What products and services could you bundle together that would complement each other, increase the value of the sale, and enhance the benefits your customer receives from conducting business with you?

GIVE YOUR CUSTOMERS OPTIONS

Years ago, Sears department stores made the "Good, Better, Best" concept of selling popular. For many of their products, especially appliances, they had three models; a "Good" model, a "Better" model, and a "Best" model.

Instead of trying to sell one product to everyone, they gave their customers choices. What about your products and services? What can you do to "categorize" your offerings as "good, better, and best?"

OTHER TOOLS

Up-selling, cross-selling and bundling are not the only tools you have at your disposal to increase the size of purchase. However, incorporating just these three techniques into your business can have a dramatic effect on your profitability.

These tools increase your sales and profits without increasing customer acquisition and marketing costs, and can immediately add 20-40% in pure profits to your bottom line.

Here are a few other tools that will help you achieve the same objective:

- **Payment Plans** – Sometimes it is difficult for customers to pay for certain products and services all at once. If you can offer payment plans you will be able to pick up sales you would have otherwise missed, and get larger volume sales that you normally wouldn't get.

- **Point of Purchase Promotions** – Often called "impulse" items, you will find these in abundance in convenience and grocery stores located around the cash register. These are items that the customer may not have been thinking of purchasing, but ends up spending extra money when the item "catches their eye" as they check out. What kind of products or services could you offer at the point of purchase?

- **Subscriptions and Continuity Programs** – Do you offer a product or service that your customers can purchase on a regular basis? Companies such as book-of-the-month clubs and CD/DVD clubs offer their programs on a regular basis. Is there anything that you can do, provide, or offer your customers that can be sold in regular intervals?

HOW TO MAKE IT WORK FOR YOU

Even though increasing the average purchase amount is the easiest way for most businesses to increase their revenues and profits; it is surprising how few put these tactics to work for them.

You may not be in the fast food business like McDonald's, but these principles apply to just about everyone. To get started creating your up-sells, cross-sells, and package deals, ask yourself these questions:

- What additional products and services would naturally complement what my customer is buying from me?
- Can I suggest to my customer that they upgrade to a better model, larger quantity, more comprehensive model, or perhaps a more frequent application?
- Could I find a way to combine multiple products and services together that would give my customers more value or enjoyment?

To be effective at increasing the size of purchase, it is important to understand what you are actually doing. You are fulfilling your obligation to your customers and clients, making certain they receive the most value, benefit and enjoyment from the products and services they purchase from you. If you have additional products and services that will enhance the value you provide, then you must give them that option.

When you present up-sells, cross-sells and package offers, it is a numbers game. Some will take advantage of your offer and some will not, but at least you have given them the opportunity to receive additional value. You haven't made the decision for them; you have given them a choice to decide for themselves. If you are sincerely trying to add value, then they won't see you as being pushy. They will see you as trying to help them get more bang for their buck. This is important to understand since your customers, clients and patients aren't really purchasing products and services from you; they are buying solutions and benefits.

Chapter 12:

Increase Profit Margins

The second growth key under the category of increasing average transaction values is to improve your profit margins.

Investopedia.com defines profit margin as "a ratio of profitability calculated as net income divided by revenues, or net profits divided by sales." Basically, it is how much out of every dollar of sales a company actually keeps in earnings.

The more steps there are in the processes from production to delivery, the more room there is for extra costs to come in, and the lower the profit margin will be. Every effort should be made to monitor, control and reduce costs whenever possible.

IMPROVING PROFIT MARGINS WITH SMART MARKETING

Everyone wants their business to make more money. The easiest way to do this is to make your marketing more effective by producing better results, making more sales, and increasing profits as much as possible. You must learn how to force every marketing dollar in your budget to work harder.

Marketing and advertising are some of the biggest wastes of money in business. By learning to be a smarter, more effective and more efficient marketer, you can eliminate the majority of your wasted marketing budget while increasing the response of your marketing efforts.

When you consider how much it "costs" in marketing expense to bring in a dollar of actual profit, it isn't hard to see why so many businesses have a difficult time showing a positive return on their marketing investment.

In this chapter, I want to address five marketing topics that can make a huge impact on improving your profit margins. These marketing topics are:

1. Your Unique Selling Proposition
2. Direct Response Marketing
3. Testing
4. Target and Niche Marketing
5. Raising Your Prices

Most of these tools are covered in detail in other chapters, so I won't repeat myself. I will touch on each topic briefly and reference the corresponding chapter in case you want to review these topics.

YOUR UNIQUE SELLING PROPOSITION

By developing a Unique Selling Proposition differentiating your business from your competitors, and integrating it into every facet of your marketing, you will improve your ability to generate quality leads that convert to paying customers at high levels.

Chapter 6 is dedicated to this topic.

DIRECT RESPONSE MARKETING

Direct response ads with enticing and compelling offers should always be used in place of traditional image advertising. Direct response marketing has the sole purpose of achieving a measureable response from your market. Because results can be measured, you can hold direct response marketing accountable for producing results in lead generation and sales.

Chapter 16 is about direct response marketing.

TESTING

Carefully testing advertisements and marketing ideas before rolling out expensive campaigns will save an incredible amount of money while increasing the results you ultimately receive.

The topic of testing was covered in Chapter 2 with "Marketing Maxim #8: Test everything and measure results."

TARGET AND NICHE MARKETING

Focus your marketing resources on highly qualified prospects in narrowly focused niche markets. This gives you the best chance of getting a high return on your marketing investment and increasing your profit margins.

Chapters 5 and 8 cover niche marketing in greater detail.

RAISE YOUR PRICES

Perhaps the easiest way to increase profit margins is to raise prices. With all other factors remaining the same, a 5% increase in price will result in a 5% increase in profit margin.

I know what you're saying: "Oh, if only it were that easy!" Actually, for some businesses, it is that easy.

The next section of this chapter will help you price your products and services for maximum profits.

PRICING TO MAXIMIZE PROFITS

The subject of pricing your products and services can get very complex. For the purpose of this book, and with the goal of increasing profit margins in mind, I am going to touch on a few important factors to consider when pricing your products and services. Those factors include:

- Pricing for your strategic objective.
- Why you should never compete on price.
- Testing prices.
- Presenting price.
- Effective discounting strategies.
- How to increase your prices.
- Pricing gimmicks that work.

PRICING FOR YOUR STRATEGIC OBJECTIVE

The pricing strategy you choose should be based on the strategic objective you wish to achieve. When it comes to pricing, there are several different strategic objectives you may have:

- Price low to capture or buy market share.
- Price low to crush the competition.
- Price to the market to be competitive.
- Price high to maximize profits.
- Price for maximum profits and sales.

The purpose of this book is maximizing business growth, so we are going to focus on the last of those objectives. When pricing for maximum profits and sales, your goal is to get the most profit possible, but not at the risk of losing customers.

THE MOST IMPORTANT THING TO KNOW ABOUT PRICE

It is important to remember that price is about *perception* of value, and has little to do with *actual* value. Your customer will buy your product or service if they believe the perceived value is greater than the price they have to pay to buy it.

The entire purpose of your marketing effort is to spread the word about your products and services and convince your market that the value is higher than the price you are asking them to pay.

WHY YOU SHOULD NEVER COMPETE ON PRICE

If you only take away one concept about pricing from this chapter, let it be this: Never compete on price. Unless you have a substantial cost advantage that will be impossible for competitors to duplicate, competing on price is a battle you will eventually lose.

I'm sure you have seen this many times: a business lowers their price, thus forcing their competitor to reduce their price a little more. This miniature "price war" continues until margins waste away. With the exception of the customer, everyone loses when this happens.

Why compete on price when there are so many ways to differentiate your business, products and services, and when there are so many ways to add value to your offering?

Instead of competing on price, become a better marketer.

TESTING PRICES

When it comes to pricing your products and services, all the theory in the world won't tell you what your optimum price is. The only way to know for certain is to let your customers tell you... and let them tell you with their wallets. It's impossible to know the best price for your product or service without testing.

On more than one occasion I have seen pricing research fail miserably. Based on focus groups, interviews and surveys, the research didn't consider that the market may say one thing when there is nothing at stake, but when they have to vote with their wallets, they may say something completely different.

Sometimes raising prices can actually increase sales. This happens when the higher price creates a higher perceived value. Many smart marketers use higher prices to cover the cost of additional bonus items or incentives that get more customers to buy. These bonuses increase the perceived value of the package offer and result in more sales.

I'm not saying that the only way to adjust price is by increasing it. Sometimes lowering prices can result in a significant increase in sales. However, it has been my experience that most companies tend to under-price their products and services.

The bottom line is this: the only way to determine your optimum price is to test.

PRESENTING PRICE

Presenting your price properly is often more important than setting the right price. The key to presenting your price is to compare it with something known to be more expensive and of perceived high value.

Here are several techniques that use the "compare and contrast" method to give the perception that your price is a great deal:

- **Monthly Installments** – Offer to let your customer pay low monthly payments instead of one large price, and then advertise the monthly installment price. A good example is in car sales: many people are more concerned about the monthly price of the car than the actual total price.
- **Individual Value Comparison** – With this method you will place an individual value on each component of a package or bundle deal. Then you add all the individual components together and compare it to the asking price.
- **"Reason Why" Method** – Sometimes it's hard for customers to understand why you charge a high or low price for your product or service. Telling the customer why the price is so high or low helps reconcile the price discrepancy and helps them accept it as reasonable.
- **Pain Avoidance** – Give your prospect a realistic picture of what it is costing them to <u>not</u> solve their problem by putting a price tag on it. Then you can compare that price to the relatively small cost of your product or service that remedies their problem.
- **"Most – Some – But" Method** – This method is used to dramatize the discounts or low price you offer compared to your competitors. It would flow like this:

Most upscale salons charge you $75 to $100.

Some salons offer specials as low as $50 to $60.

But our preferred customer price is just $39.95

Discounting can be a very valuable tool to assist in closing sales. However, too many sales people and companies over-use and abuse this tactic. Instead of discounting, consider building value by adding low cost, high value bonuses and premiums to persuade your customers to buy.

With that said, if you are going to use a discount, be sure to attach a deadline to the offer to create a sense of urgency to act now. Here are a few effective discounting strategies you can test in your business:

- **New Product Introduction Discount** – When you introduce a new product you may consider offering it to a select group at a special introductory price.
- **Quantity-Tiered Discount** – The discount increases based on the volume of the purchase. For example, if you purchase 3 units, you get a 10% discount; 10 units and you get a 15% discount; and 20 units gets you a 20% discount off the regular price.
- Package Discount – You offer a lower total price for a package (or bundle) of products or services. The total value of the entire package of goods and services should be worth more than their individual prices added up.

HOW TO INCREASE PRICES

Increasing your prices can be tricky. A public price increase can disrupt your customer's purchasing behavior. Here are 7 ways to increase your prices without causing a big stir:

- Decrease the discounts you offer to your customers.
- Increase the minimum order sizes that customers must meet to receive discounts.

- Start selling higher margin products and services while phasing out lower margin items.
- Increase your delivery charge and start charging for any special services related to delivery.
- Bill customers for engineering and installation services that you previously included in the purchase price.
- Raise prices for any overtime worked on rush orders.
- Write stiff penalty clauses into all your contracts.

CONCLUSION

Pricing is a major factor in successfully marketing and selling your products and services. Regardless of the price you choose, make certain that you have a carefully planned objective in mind and that your pricing strategy supports your objective.

Ultimately, your ability to raise your prices is simply a perception of value. When you build value into your offering, you are able to charge higher prices. Just make sure that you test your price points or you may end up missing out on a lot of potential profits.

CUTTING COSTS TO GROW YOUR BUSINESS

Knowing and controlling where your money is going is critical. As a business leader you need to stay abreast of expenditures, with money being spent only after careful analysis of how it will contribute to your bottom line profits.

THE PROBLEM WITH CUTTING COSTS

I've met quite a few entrepreneurs and business leaders that approach cutting costs as a key to improving profitability. There is nothing wrong with cutting waste and improving efficiency, but

I'm unaware of any single business that has ever made a fortune by cutting costs alone.

Improving profit margins is only one of the Nine Growth Keys, and cutting costs is only one way to improve profit margins. If your goal is to grow, don't let yourself get distracted for too long by cutting costs. Stay focused on your growth goals while constantly striving to improve each of the Nine Growth Keys.

Entrepreneurs and executives trying to cut costs in their businesses often take it out of their marketing budgets. Remember what you learned in the first chapter from Peter Drucker? Marketing is one of only two functions in your business that produces results. Why would you cut a business function that's an investment in your growth? Don't make the mistake of looking at marketing is an expense.

Chapter 13:

Increase the Number of Purchases

The next growth key in the TriFecta Exponential Growth Model is to get your customers to buy from you more often.

If you want your customers to purchase from you more often, then you must give them good reasons to do so. You can't just hope that they will think of you the next time they need your products or services. That would put you in a very weak and vulnerable position. You need to have a strategic and proactive plan to bring customers back to you on a consistent basis.

This is important for you to understand, because the longer your customers go between purchases from your business, the higher the chance that they will buy from your competition.

There have been numerous studies dedicated to understanding this concept. One recent study reported that for **every month you don't have meaningful contact with your customer, you lose about 10% of your top-of-mind awareness**. This means that your customers can completely forget about you in less than a year!

Consider how much money the average business spends to acquire customers. There are advertising costs, marketing costs, and that doesn't even include the salaries and commissions you pay your sales staff. The old saying, "out of sight, out of mind", holds true in the business world, and you can't afford to let that happen to you. Not only must you constantly stay in contact with your customers, it must be <u>meaningful</u> contact. Meaningful contact includes educational information, notices of sales and special promotions, introduction of new items, and special incentives and other offers that may benefit them.

THE IMPORTANCE OF INCREASING THE NUMBER OF PURCHASES

Too many businesses operate with a one-time sale mentality, not putting enough of their marketing efforts on repeat sales. But the "back-end" is where the real money is. It costs 5-8 times more to get a new customer to buy from you than it does to get an existing customer to buy from you again. When you see it that way, it makes perfect sense to spend the majority of your time, effort and marketing dollars strengthening the relationships you already have with your existing customers.

If you have been in business for more than a couple of years, your existing customer base is the most powerful source of profits you have.

Increasing the average number of purchases of your average customer is both a growth key and a growth multiplier. Improving this growth key by our goal of just 15% would have a tremendous impact on your business, especially combined with the other growth keys.

THE REAL MONEY IS IN THE BACK-END

There are many very successful businesses that lose money on the customers they generate from their advertising efforts. In other words, the amount of profits actually generated from the customers produced by the ad is much lower than the cost to buy the ad, fill the order, and the general overhead of the business. The end result is that the cost of acquiring the customer is greater than the profits generated.

These businesses can be incredibly profitable, because the real money to be made is generated in the back-end, or repeat sales. It doesn't matter if your back-end consists of selling your customers additional products and services, or if they re-purchase the same products and services over again. The important point to understand is that the more times you get your customers to do business with you, the more opportunities you will have to make a profit from that customer.

When you properly structure and manage your back-end sales program, you can increase your profits substantially while simultaneously increasing your customer satisfaction and loyalty. Ultimately, your objective is to "program" or "condition" your customers to purchase more frequently, and this represents one of the most simple and effective ways to increase your profits.

What if you don't have additional products and services to sell your customers? That doesn't mean that you can't have a profitable back-end to your business. Are there other businesses or organizations that have products and services that would naturally complement what you sell, and provide additional benefits or enhancements to your customers? If so, you could recommend those to your customers for a "commission", or percentage of sales.

BUILDING YOUR DATABASE

Creating a database of current, past and prospective customers is the first step in increasing customer purchase frequency. There are many things you need to know about your customers and prospects, and a database is the most efficient way to collect and manage this data.

When building your database, think about what you need to know about your three groups of customers: current customers, inactive customers, and prospective customers. What questions do you need to answer in order to market to them properly?

Who are your current customers? You need records that show who they are, what products and services they have purchased, when and what their last purchase was, and how frequently they purchase from you.

Who are your inactive customers? When is the last time they purchased from you? Have they sent any referrals to you? Are they using your competitors?

Who are your prospective customers? Do you know who they are? Have you developed an "Ideal Customer Profile" accurately describing who they are so you can target your marketing efforts at them? Do you have a list of them, and do you know how to reach them? Are you reaching them on a regular basis?

The answer to these questions gives you powerful information that you can use to grow your business. If you're not currently using a computer database to keep track of this and other customer information, you should be. Consider your database the starting point to significant profits.

CAPTURING CONTACT INFORMATION FROM YOUR CUSTOMERS

If a business were to lose all their equipment, inventory, employees, etc., but still maintain their list of customers, they could rebuild. The most valuable asset any business has is not the products or services they sell, their equipment, computer systems, staff, or their location. The most valuable asset any business has is their database of customers.

However, if a business was to lose all their customers, think of all the costs in time, money, and effort it would take to rebuild. Replacing a database of people with whom you have developed relationships, trust, confidence, and loyalty is an enormous and costly undertaking.

What systems do you currently have in place to store or capture the contact data of your customers and prospects? Not only should you have your current and past customers listed in an easily segmented and searchable database, you should also be capturing the contact information of everyone who visits your business or enquires about your products and services.

You could have a sign-up sheet in your place of business for people who wish to be added to your list to receive special offers and sales. You can have the same on your website. Remember the lead generation mechanism mentioned in Chapter 7? Put it to work for you in growing your database.

Make certain you have some type of system in place to collect contact information of people interested in your business, products or services. If you don't, then you are losing a lot of money.

FOLLOWING UP WITH YOUR DATABASE

There are many things you can do to make your efforts in selling additional products and services to your database of customers more effective. It's not difficult to do, but it does require a little planning, thought and creativity. But more than anything else, it requires taking action.

What can you do to bring your customers back to your business more often? What can you do to build customer loyalty and encourage them to send you referrals?

There are several things you need to consider when creating your follow up program, and the first is how many times you want to contact your clients over a period of time. You want them to know that you are thinking of them, but the last thing you want to do is become a nuisance. Remember, your communication with them needs to offer value.

How frequently should you contact your customers with communications of value? That will vary depending on your business, but a good rule of thumb is to contact them once per month. Remember, for each month your customers don't receive meaningful communication from you, you lose 10% of your top-of-mind awareness.

Next, you need to decide how you will contact your database. What method of contact has the greatest chance of getting their attention? What method is most cost-effective? What method of contact provides the greatest likelihood of them responding?

You have several options, including letters, postcards, faxes, newsletters, email, phone calls, and in-person visits. Each of these methods of contact should be carefully considered before creating your follow up campaign. My suggestion is to mix it up. When you use the same method over and over, it can become too common and response rates will drop.

Now you need to determine the purpose of contacting them. Are you going to thank them for being your customer? Is it to make them an offer on new merchandise or services they may need? Maybe you can involve them in a referral contest or promotion? Remember, your database should tell you each of your customers's buying habits and patterns, so you can make offers specific to their needs.

There are many "personal" reasons for you to contact your customers, and I recommend adding some to your follow up program. Some of these personal reasons can include:

- Birthday and anniversary cards and offers.
- Postcards or letters on the anniversary of their first purchase from you.
- A questionnaire or survey asking for their opinion and evaluation of your products and services.

Keeping in touch with your customers is one of the best marketing tools you will ever have, and it can be very simple to do. The important point to remember is that all three groups of your customers (current, past and prospective) need to be nurtured to maximize the growth of your business.

OTHER TOOLS FOR INCREASING THE NUMBER OF PURCHASES

Other than your customer database, there are dozens of additional tools you can use to keep your customers coming back to you. I'm sure that you can think of a number of things you can do in your business that will help you develop trust and loyalty, both critical factors in getting your customers to come back to you again and again. Here are a just a few to get you started:

- Customer surveys
- Create a "Wow!" factor
- Establish a frequent buyer's club
- Company newsletter
- Superior customer service
- Over deliver on your promise
- Service contracts
- In-package advertisement inserts
- In-store signs
- Create a continuity program
- Statement stuffers
- Gift certificates

CONCLUSION

The single most important marketing strategy and system that you must create to maximize the growth of your business is to communicate on a regular basis with your customers, prospects and vendors. While it is not a difficult strategy to understand or implement, it is neglected by far too many businesses.

Chapter 14:

Reduce Customer Attrition

The next growth key that increases customer purchase frequency is to reduce customer attrition. Simply stated, customer attrition is the opposite of customer retention; it is how many customers you lose over a period of time.

The average business loses about 20% of their customers annually. Companies doing nothing to prevent customer attrition or increase retention can have attrition rates much higher.

WHY DO CUSTOMERS LEAVE?

With the average business losing one out of five customers annually, we must examine the reasons why this is happening. Statistics released by the US Small Business Administration and the US Chamber of Commerce reveal very interesting and troublesome data:

- 1% dies.

- 3% move outside of their local geographical area (20-25% move annually, but most stay nearby).
- 5% seek alternative solutions.
- 9% are lured away by competitors.
- 14% are dissatisfied with the product or service.
- 68% are unhappy with customer service).

This research shows that 82% of the customers you lose are unhappy. Unfortunately, unhappy customers usually don't complain… they just leave without ever giving you a chance to make things right.

A study from the Research Institute of America found that 96% of your unsatisfied customers will never say anything to you about their discontent.

But it gets worse. Not only does losing these unhappy customers drive up acquisition costs, but it is costing you potential lost sales. The same study found that unhappy customers tell at least nine others about their bad experience, thus jeopardizing even more potential sales.

PERCEPTION OR REALITY?

Why do your customers leave? Your perception of the reasons why customers leave you may not be the reality. Research conducted by RightNow Technologies found there are huge discrepancies in the reasons a company's sales force and management team thinks their customers leave, and the actual reason customers leave.

- 73% of customers leave because they are dissatisfied with the service they received from a company. However, company management believes only 21% of their customers leave because of customer service.

- Management believes that 48% of their customers leave for better pricing. The research found that only 25% of customers leave for pricing reasons.

In their book *"Leading on the Edge of Chaos"*, authors Emmet and Mark Murphy shared some enlightening statistics:

- It costs five to eight times more to get a new customer than it does to resell an existing customer.
- A 2% increase in customer retention has the same effect as decreasing costs by 10%.
- 74% of so-called "loyal" customers will buy outside of their favorite brands.
- Customer profitability tends to increase over the life of a retained customer.

HOW CUSTOMER ATTRITION AFFECTS YOUR BUSINESS

As previously noted, the average business loses about 20% of their customers each year. That one simple fact explains why so many businesses are struggling today. It's why they have to put so much money, effort and time into attracting new customers to do business with them.

As a business owner, entrepreneur or manager, it is very important to understand what customer attrition is costing your business. Let's do the math together…

- 20% customer attrition equates to 100% customer turnover every five years.
- If all you did was reduce customer attrition by 50%, your business would double in 10 years.

- To achieve just a 10% increase in sales you must add a 30% increase in customers.

The affects customer attrition has on your business are profound, but look at what reducing customer attrition can do for profits...

> "An increase in customer retention of 5% can yield an increase in profits of 25-125%."
>
> **Frederick Reichheld**
> Author of "*The Loyalty Effect*"

Gaining new customers is costly, and in many cases, the money earned on the first sale doesn't even cover customer acquisition costs. In fact, studies have shown that it is 16 times easier to sell to an existing customer than to a new one.

Why would any business owner, manager, salesperson or entrepreneur spend a minute of time or a dollar of their resources attracting new customers before doing all they can to reactivate past customers and clients? Again, the real money and profits come from additional sales of your products and services to your existing customers, or the back-end.

MOVE YOUR CUSTOMERS UP THE LOYALTY LADDER

There is an excellent book called *Up the Loyalty Ladder* by Murray and Neil Raphel. You will see a diagram of the Loyalty Ladder on the next page. The Raphels point out that the market is made up of the following groups of people:

Suspects - There are many suspects and they are made up of people, organizations, or companies that have never done business with you, but that may have a need or want for your products or services at a future date. At this point, however, they are not yet identified.

Prospects - The next group, prospects, have somehow shown an interest in what you are selling by responding to an ad, answering an inquiry, or calling your business.

Shoppers - These are people actively searching for what you offer, and they are making efforts to get to know the benefits of buying your products or services, and in doing business with you. They have a need or a want, and if you can show them clear advantages of doing business with you, they will move up to the next rung of the ladder to becoming a Customer.

Customers – These are people who have made some type of purchase from you. Unfortunately, this is where many business owners assume that because someone has purchased from them and is now "in the books", they don't have to pay particular attention to them. But that is not the case at all. In fact, quite the contrary is true. This is the time to nurture and develop that relationship with your customer. If you don't, your customer can very easily slip away to do business with your competitor.

The Loyalty Ladder

170

Moving your customers up the Loyalty Ladder to Raving Fan status isn't that difficult, but it doesn't happen by itself. It takes a well-planned and well-executed effort on your part. It is very unfortunate that most businesses either don't understand this concept, or they aren't implementing marketing programs to convert their Clients into Raving Fans. While this is very unfortunate for them, it represents a great opportunity for you.

Do you have a plan for moving people up the Loyalty Ladder? Do you have marketing systems in place that effectively lead people from Suspect, to Prospect, to Shopper, and then on to becoming a Customer?

Once they are a customer, do you continue to move them up the ladder to Client, then to Advocate, and finally converting them to a Raving Fan?

Marketing is leadership, and you must take full responsibility for leading your prospects and customers up the Loyalty Ladder to becoming Raving Fans.

HOW TO REDUCE CUSTOMER ATTRITION

The majority of businesses don't know what their customer attrition rate is, much less what to do about it. So the first step in transforming your business is to find out what your attrition rate is and which clients are no longer actively buying from you. Once you know who and how many customers that have stopped buying from you, then you can do something about it.

Imagine your customers are in a leaking bucket. If you don't plug the holes you will be continuously pouring new clients into your bucket only to lose them again. That is why you need to have a customer attrition prevention system in place.

Contacting your old customers by phone can be a very effective way of determining why your customers leave you in the first place. Just be sure to make the phone call very personal. If you can't do it by phone, then a personal letter can work. An important point to remember is that you should always start with the most recently inactive clients and customers, as these are the most likely to become active again.

Once you have your "reasons why", then you must begin plugging those leaks in the bucket. Whatever those reasons are, create a plan to make certain they don't happen again.

THE CUSTOMER NEWSLETTER

When a customer stops dealing with a company, it becomes easy for them to forget about that company altogether. Newsletters are effective at keeping in touch with your customers and moving them up the Loyalty Ladder to Raving Fan status.

The best newsletter is the one you personally write and produce. It comes directly from you, can be written in a very personal style, and can cover topics of direct interest to the people who do business with you.

You can also purchase newsletters from outside sources that print your name and company information on them, and mail them for you. Some of these newsletters are better than others, and most are general in nature. If you use one of these sources, make sure you can contribute at least one custom article per issue.

Don't worry too much about what to put in your newsletter, as there is no shortage of information. Just keep the content relevant, informative, interesting, and useful to your target market.

Your newsletter doesn't have to be long or complicated. A simple four-page, front and back newsletter will do nicely. This can be printed on an 11" x 17" piece of paper, folded in the middle to make it four 8.5" x 11" pages in a booklet format. Fold it again and it can be ready for mailing. These are simple, easy to create, and don't take much time.

If you are not already using your own personal newsletter, you really should consider it. There are not many things you can do that are as effective as keeping in touch with your customers and prospects while providing them usable and educational information. Additionally, it is a non-threatening, non-salesy way to promote your business and your products and services.

TOOLS TO REDUCE CUSTOMER ATTRITION

Many of the tools you should use to reduce customer attrition have already been discussed in this book. Allow me to include a quick review, as well as introduce you to a few more.

- **Create a customer communication program** – this topic was covered in detail in Chapter 13, under the section of "Following Up with Your Database."
- **Excel at customer service** - Excellent customer service doesn't just happen, and it is much more than a concept or a catchphrase. Delivering quality customer service is something that you need to think about and plan very carefully and train your employees to achieve.
- **Implement a customer reactivation program** - It pays to try to win your inactive customers back. Do this by developing a customer reactivation program like the one discussed in Chapter 10.
- **Deliver more than expected** – Always deliver a little more than you promised and you will never lose. If you under-deliver on what you promise, the result will be a lost customer.

- **Create longevity perks** – Most people will not develop a sense of belonging to your organization until you make an issue of it. Reward your customers when they remain your customers for certain amounts of time.

- **Post purchase reassurance** - Reinforce the customer's feelings about their purchase. Tell them they are smart shoppers, got a great deal, and that they have great taste. Tell them why they are lucky to have what they bought. People need to know that they made the right decision, especially after the purchase of a big-ticket item.

- **Prearrange future sales** - Once you've made a sale, can you lay the groundwork for future sales, or a future cross-sell? This secures a customer before they have any chance to go elsewhere. Send them a postcard, newsletter, or something that reminds them of when it's time to come in and purchase again.

- **Customer newsletters** – Every business should have a customer newsletter. Used properly, it's a powerful, non-threatening tool that can provide a lot of useful information and education to your customers. Make sure that you provide valuable information in your newsletter to keep it from looking like "just another sales brochure."

- **Customer appreciation events** - Throw a party for your best customers. It can be a cocktail party, a barbecue, or anything else that lets them have a good time. It's a great way to promote yourself and do something nice for your customers.

- **Preferred customer sales and discounts** - Offer exclusive opportunities to receive special "insider deals" as a reward for being one of your best customers.
  - **Sneak previews** - A great way to make your best customers feel special is to invite them to closed-door previews of your new products.

Chapter 15:

Extend Customer's Buying Lifetime

The final growth key that you need to understand is extending your customer's "buying lifetime." You may know this as "customer retention."

It makes logical sense that the longer a customer continues to do business with you, the more products and services you will have the opportunity to sell them. This, of course, translates into more revenues and profits for your business.

For example, let's say your average customer purchases from you for a period of five years before moving on to one of your competitors, or they no longer needs the products and services your business offers. If you could extend that five years by just one year, that would translate into an increase in profits of 20%. On top of that, the longer the customer's buying lifetime with you, the more chances you will have of getting referrals from them of others who can use and benefit from the products and services you sell.

YOUR MOST VALUABLE BUSINESS ASSET

Most business owners know exactly how much money they have invested and tied up in furniture, inventory and equipment. They can tell you how old it is, how much it has depreciated and what the remaining life expectancy is. This information is important to know.

What I find interesting is that very few business owners and managers know what the value of their most important asset is... and that is their customers.

Does your marketing program have systems in place to extend the life of your most valuable business asset? What exactly are you doing to prevent your customers from defecting to your competition? I can promise you that your competitors would love to take your customers, so extending your customer's buying lifetime is something you must work on.

Are your customers thrilled about the products you offer and the services you provide? How do you know? Have you asked them recently? Do you have a system in place to find out?

Notice in the last paragraph that I used the word "thrilled", not "satisfied." There's a big difference between being thrilled and being satisfied.

Last year more than 200 million Americans stopped doing business with companies they were "satisfied" with. Additionally, 60% of so-called "satisfied" customers switch companies and brands on a regular basis. You can't afford not to "thrill" your customers, because the cost of losing your customers is too high.

RELATIONSHIP BUYERS

Dr. Paul Wang is a Professor at Northwestern University in Chicago and one of the world's foremost experts on database marketing. Dr. Wang reports that there are two types of buyers: "transaction" buyers and "relationship" buyers.

The transaction buyer is only interested in price and has no loyalty toward any business. They will leave you for your competitor to save a dollar. They spend hours researching prices on the internet, call all of your competitors for quotes, can afford to "wait out" a negotiation, and take pride in getting the best deal or lowest price.

Relationship buyers look for advisors, salespeople and businesses they feel they can trust. They want friendly companies with reliable products. They want to buy from people who will remember them, do favors for them, and who will build a relationship with them. When they find this person or business they will gladly give them all of their business.

Relationship buyers know they could save a dollar or two by shopping around, but they find the process wastes too much of their time and energy. If you treat them properly, relationship buyers will stay with you forever.

According to Dr. Wang, every company and every salesperson has a base of "relationship" buyers.

Transaction buyers give you very little profit. Because they only buy when they get the lowest prices, the margins on their sales are much lower than the margins on relationship buyers' sales.

Studies have found that about 15-20% of customers are transaction buyers, while 80-85% are relationship buyers who generate most of the profits.

Since relationship buyers are the ones who stay with you for the long haul, you want to do everything you can to make them happy.

HOW TO EXTEND YOUR CUSTOMER'S BUYING LIFETIME

Lengthening the amount of time your customers do business with you is a sure way to increase your profits. If you were able to increase the buying lifetime of your average customer from three years to four years, you just increased your profits by 33.3%.

The formula for keeping your customers longer is actually very simple, and can be broken down into three components:

1. Communicate regularly with your customers.
2. Offer them products and services they want.
3. Provide excellent customer service.

COMMUNICATE REGULARLY WITH YOUR CUSTOMERS

I'm going to repeat myself here, but only because it is such an important point. To extend the lifetime of your customers, it is imperative to have frequent and consistent communications of value and meaning with them. Your customers need to hear from you in some way at least once per month.

I will also reiterate that when it comes to communicating with customers, the old adage of "out of sight, out of mind" is true. But so is "out of hearing, out of mind", as well as "out of reading, out of mind."

Don't make the mistake of thinking that you and your business are important to them. You are not their spouse, child, or their best friend. You need to give them reasons to think of you in a positive light on a regular basis, or you will be forgotten. When they need the product or service you offer, they may buy it from you, but they may buy it from someone else because they have forgotten about you.

Make certain all of your communications are "meaningful" communications. Keep your communications customer-focused. Keep their best interests in mind. If there is a special sale or a new product or service you think they would want to know about, by all means let them know.

Consistent communication of value is necessary for you to remain *fresh* in your customer's mind.

Let's take a closer look at the word "fresh" as it relates to communication with your customers and prospects. Fresh means something new. It can mean new products and services, or it could be a new idea. Always keep your communications fresh.

If it is impossible to continually freshen your product and service line, you could provide your customers with offers from joint venture partners. Though the products and services may come from your joint venture partner, when you introduce your customers to a special deal that will be beneficial to them, you will be appreciated… and you can make some nice, new profits for your endorsement.

Another communication idea that will extend the buying lifetime of your customers is to make survey calls. Survey calls are a very effective way to collect customer data, and an indirect way to sell.

You need to understand what your customers want, need, and will buy from you. In learning what your customers want and need, you subtly let them know that you care about them, and you have their best interest in mind. This creates a strong impression.

Survey calls will always give you valuable information about how to extend the life of your customer, but as a bonus, it will usually drive additional sales.

OFFER PRODUCTS AND SERVICES THEY WANT

To extend the buying lifetime of your customers, you need to be able to provide them with a continuous stream of offers. If you only provide a limited number of products and services, then you will have to get creative.

What types of offers could you make that would provide added benefit to your customers?

You could provide enhanced pricing options such as a discount for long-term pre-payments, or you could create new packages of previously separate products and services. What about offering larger quantities or bigger bundles?

Think of all the marketing tools we have already covered in this book, such as increasing purchase frequency, back-end sales, and cross-selling. All of these offers will help you extend the purchasing life of your customer. If you continue delivering value and ensuring your customers are thrilled with their purchases, there is no reason for them to ever leave.

Can you make longer-term offers, or offers that get realized over a longer period of time? Examples of these could be subscription, continuity or membership offers.

What about offering an upgrade program? Upgrades are a powerful way to get people to buy from you again. Consider software manufacturers such as Microsoft and Intuit. A significant part of their business model is based on getting their customers to purchase upgrades and updates. Actually, you could say that Intuit (creators of TurboTax, Quicken and QuickBooks) has built their entire business around the concept of updates.

How could you use the concept of upgrades? Could you upgrade to an improved delivery mode? What about enhanced interaction, communication or support?

You have heard it a thousand times before, "under promise, over deliver." It is essential to success in business, but it is also often overlooked. Too many businesses do exactly the opposite – over promise and under deliver – and then wonder why they have problems.

Show your customers how much you appreciate them. Telling them is important, but a better way would be to show them. There are many simple and low-cost things you can do to let them know they are not "just another sale."

As part of your communication program, consider adding small appreciation gifts such as movie passes, gift certificates, and special arrangements with local professionals such as accountants, consultants and attorneys. You could offer them free consultations and other low-cost products or services.

YOUR BEST CUSTOMERS ARE YOUR COMPETITOR'S BEST PROSPECTS

Right now your competition is making plans and taking steps to take your best customers away from you. And if it were up to them, they would also try to prevent you from getting any new ones. It's not malicious... it's just business.

What are you going to do about it?

Constantly communicate value and show appreciation to all of your customers. Don't let them forget about you.

Chapter 16:

Use Only Direct Response

The investment required for successful media advertising can be very high for small and medium-sized businesses. Often entrepreneurs and business executives give media advertising a shot, but find they don't get any return on their investment. They end up frustrated and quit.

As I mentioned in a previous chapter, the most common reason businesses fail with advertising is that they are not doing the right *type* of advertising in the first place. They are running Image Advertising when they need to run Direct Response Advertising. Very often media sales reps and advertising agencies sell businesses on the concept of advertising for "brand building" purposes. They are told that if they don't advertise, then their competitors will beat them to their customers.

I cannot argue with this statement because it could *possibly* be true. However, not only is it not *necessarily* true, but it's very likely not true at all.

I recommend to all small and medium-sized businesses that all of their advertising should be direct response. The purpose of direct response is to do just that: direct a response of some kind. This response can be in the form of a purchase from your store, a request for more information or a free consultation, etc. Because the purpose is to generate a response of some kind, direct response advertising can be measured and held accountable for results.

The majority of advertising that you see in any media is image advertising, and it doesn't ask for any instant or direct response. These ads often look exactly the same as all the other ads: the company name is the headline of the ad, there is very little copy on the ad, lots of "white" space, and there is no incentive to respond immediately. There is no way of knowing how effective your ads are because you have no way of measuring the response. Therefore, you have no way of calculating your return on investment for the advertisement.

If your ads look like what I described, do yourself a favor and stop running them now! You are wasting your money.

Another reason image advertising is a waste of money is that your prospects and customers don't really care about you or your business. All they care about is how you can help them. Stop running image ads!

Image advertising can help build brand awareness, and this is important for large companies like Coca-Cola and Nike who have enormous advertising budgets. However, most small and mid-sized businesses can't afford to spend their money this way.

THINK OF YOUR ADVERTISING AS A SALESPERSON

Would you hire someone to go door-to-door handing out business cards? The card has your company name, address, and phone number on it, and hopefully what you sell is made evident somewhere on the card via a company name or slogan. If this salesperson were paid a base salary, wouldn't you agree that this would be a waste of money, and that you should find a better rep that will do a little more "selling?"

Yet that is exactly what image advertising is. It is a sales rep saying "Hi, I'm with Acme Widget Company. Call me if you need widgets." Just as you would demand more from your sales reps, you should demand more from your advertising.

Wouldn't you rather have a salesperson that generates immediate sales and leads? Or would you prefer a salesperson that builds brand awareness with the hope that sometime in the future someone will remember your company and call you?

Because direct response ads require a person to take a specific action, you can tell whether or not it is profitable to run that ad again, or if it needs changing to make it more effective. Additionally, direct response techniques can be effectively integrated into the marketing efforts of nearly any business, taking the form of print advertising, mail order, radio, television ads, and telemarketing.

There are many great books and resources on writing direct response ads. Be sure to take me up on the "Bonus Offer" at the end of this book and I will make sure you get several of those resources free of cost.

Start running ads that direct an immediate response that you can monitor, track and test. Image advertising merely tells your market that your company is there, so you cannot measure results. While the expense of the ad is real, the return on investment is unknown, and probably almost nothing.

The reason you run an advertisement is the same reason you are in business – to make a profit. You are not in business just to

tell your market how wonderful you and your products and
services are. Change your advertising efforts from a cost to an
investment with a measurable return. Use only direct response. It
can add significantly to your bottom line, and it will be one of the
best marketing moves you will ever make.

COMPONENTS OF A GOOD DIRECT RESPONSE AD:

- Powerful, benefit-laden headlines and sub-headlines.
- Lots of copy written in a personal style.
- A powerful offer.
- Your USP.
- Selling of the benefits, not the features.
- Use of testimonials.
- A reason to respond immediately.
- A free bonus for responding.
- Reply mechanisms.
- Advertisement response is measurable, and you can hold the ad
  accountable for results.

Chapter 17:

Your Growth Potential

Now you should have a solid understanding of the TriFecta Exponential Growth Model and the business building principles that drive it. These principles include:

- The Nine Growth Keys
- Marketing Synergy
- Compounding
- Exponential Growth

Using the Nine Growth Keys, you will find many opportunities to improve your sales and marketing efforts, the revenues generated from those efforts, and the profits you can put in your bank account. There are literally hundreds of tools and tactics you can make work for you. In fact, you will probably find there are more opportunities than there is time to work on them. Don't let this dilemma delay you from getting started.

Ultimately it comes down to this: how many of the Nine Growth Keys are you able to improve, and how many marketing tools can you put to use in your business.

I have noticed three traits shared by companies that are successful at implementing changes and improvements:

1. They have the desire to grow and improve.
2. They take the initiative to learn about better technologies and methods.
3. They take action, implementing what they learn in a systematic way.

Almost every business owner, entrepreneur, executive, and sales professional I know has attended seminars, purchased training programs, and read books and articles about building and improving their business. Unfortunately, 95% don't implement what they learn and end up frustrated and angry.

The most common problem that most companies have with implementation is that they fail to focus on one single growth key and marketing tactic at a time. They try to do too many things at once, and the result is that nothing gets accomplished.

MAKING THE TRIFECTA EXPONENTIAL GROWTH MODEL WORK FOR YOU

I want you to think about the growth potential of your business for a moment. What would be the result of applying the single most impactful concept or tactic that you learned about in this book? If you only improved one category within the TriFecta of Business Growth by 5%, what would that mean to your business? If you have a $1,000,000 business, that would mean $50,000 more in additional revenue.

If you continued to implement that idea for the next 10 years, that would total $500,000. That is half a million dollars from the implementation of just one idea!

What if you could implement one new idea each year? Or, better yet, one new idea each month? Does that seem too difficult to do? If each idea resulted in a 5% improvement in revenues, your million dollar business would grow to $6 million dollars in 10 years.

I can't promise you that you are going to achieve a 5% improvement each time you implement a new marketing idea, but even if half of them produced no result at all, wouldn't it still be worth it?

The point is that you have to start somewhere. Pick a growth key and make an improvement. Then move on to a new growth key and make an improvement. The results you will realize over time are significant, and there is no reason you can't continue doing this forever.

When you base your marketing program on the TriFecta Exponential Growth Model and work continually to improve each of the Nine Growth Keys, you engineer purpose and direction into your marketing program. That purpose is maximizing the growth of your business.

FOCUS ON ACHIEVING EXPONENTIAL GROWTH

When you build a Comprehensive Marketing Program based on the Nine Growth Keys, you will have dozens of different marketing tools and tactics driving your business toward achieving exponential growth.

Have you heard the term "leverage" used in financial talk? Leverage means to multiply the productivity of a resource. The concept of leverage isn't just limited to finance, it applies to marketing, too.

A marketing example of leverage would be getting an advertisement you are running to produce a 10% greater result. Maybe all you do is change the headline, the offer, or the placement of the ad, but the result is 10% greater productivity for your efforts for no additional cost.

There are literally hundreds of different marketing tactics and tools you can put to work for your business and almost all of them can be leveraged to produce greater results. Again, when you focus your efforts on improving each of the Nine Growth Keys, you will achieve Marketing Synergy and exponential growth.

As a business leader or entrepreneur, continue to make incremental improvements to the marketing tools and tactics driving each of the Nine Growth Keys. Even if those improvements are just a couple of percentage points each, when you get all growth keys working together, they can drive your sales through the roof.

ACHIEVING YOUR GROWTH POTENTIAL

The ultimate goal when implementing the TriFecta Exponential Growth Model is to get as many growth keys and marketing tools as you can working in concert to produce incredible improvements in sales and profits. The beauty of the model is that you don't have to be perfect to achieve great results. You just have to be steady in your progress. You have to pick a growth key and implement a marketing tactic. As you keep executing, small changes and improvements will build upon each other resulting in big improvements in your business. Remember, if you are able to make 10% improvements in each of the five growth multipliers, your business can more than double.

SIMPLE GROWTH CALCULATOR

	Now	+10%
Leads Generated	1200	1320
Conversion Rate	20%	22%
Total Number of Sales Closed	**240**	**290.4**
Yearly Purchases per Customer	10	11
Total Number of Purchases	**2,400**	**3,194.4**
Size of Purchase	$ 50	$ 55
Total Gross Sales	**$ 120,000**	**$ 175,692**
Profit Margins	50%	55%
Total Profits	**$ 60,000**	**$ 96,630.60**

What does a 10% improvement actually mean? If you are generating 100 leads per month now, it would simple be an increase to 110 per month. Does that seem impossible?

If you are currently closing 20% of those prospects, a 10% improvement would raise conversion to 22%. Based on the tools you learned in Chapter 8, doesn't that seem plausible?

Profit margins take a little more effort than the other growth multipliers, but a 10% improvement would take you from 50% to 55%. If you just raised your prices by 10%, would your customers object? Research shows that 75-80% wouldn't.

Using the different marketing tactics discussed in Chapter 11, do you think you could increase your average size of purchase from $50 to $55? I bet you can.

With just 10% improvements in these areas, your annual revenues would grow by 46.41%, and your profits would increase by 61.05%. What if you could only do half of that? It is still very significant growth, and it is well worth the time and effort, wouldn't you agree?

Would you like to see what doubling your business looks like? Take a minute to fill out the following growth calculators. In the first calculator, put your current numbers for each of the growth multipliers in the "Now" column. In the next column, improve your results by 10% and write those numbers in the appropriate boxes.

SIMPLE GROWTH CALCULATOR – 10% IMPROVEMENTS

	Now	+10%
Leads Generated		
Conversion Rate		
Total Number of Sales Closed		
Yearly Purchases per Customer		
Total Number of Purchases		
Size of Purchase		
Total Gross Sales		
Profit Margins		
Total Profits		

Maybe those numbers are too hard to believe, and you would like to insert something more realistic to you. No problem, here's another simple growth calculator to play with.

This time you decide on the percentage of increase you can make for each of the five growth multipliers. Just as before, put your current numbers in the "Now" column. In the middle column insert the percentage rate of improvement that you believe you can make using both the tools you learned about in this book, and any other tools you have in your sales and marketing toolbox. Use the far right column to record your results.

SIMPLE GROWTH CALCULATOR

	Now	(+%)	Total
Leads Generated			
Conversion Rate			
Total Number of Sales Closed			

Yearly Purchases per Customer			
Total Number of Purchases			

Size of Purchase			
Total Gross Sales			

Profit Margins			
Total Profits			

How did it turn out for you? Even if you only made 5% improvements in each of the growth multipliers, the total growth achieved would be 27.63%. There's a lot of businesses I know of that would be happy with that type of annual growth.

FREE ONLINE GROWTH CALCULATORS

If you would like to play around a little more with an automated version of these growth calculators, visit my website at

www.TriFectaMarketing.com and click on the "Free Stuff" section of the top navigation. Once you are on the "Resources and Free Stuff" page, click on the icon or link titled "Growth Calculators." If you would rather just type in the long URL, just type in the following in your favorite web browser:

"**www.TriFectaMarketing.com/growth-calculators.html**".

On this page you will find both the Simple Growth Calculator and the comprehensive Exponential Growth Calculator that I introduced you to in Chapter 4. Play around with the numbers and see what you get.

TAKING ACTION

Would you like to know the secret to being successful with the TriFecta Exponential Growth Model? It really isn't very mysterious. Here it is...

Take action... and make constant forward progress.

The main reason most businesses fail to grow or produce significant profits is that they don't do any marketing. When they do some sort of marketing, it is usually just an ineffective image advertisement given to the first media rep that wears them down.

Too many business owners and entrepreneurs falsely believe that all they have to do is open their doors for business and customers will find them. Other times, they think that if they create a superior product or service, the world will beat the proverbial path to their door. Even if you have the most incredible product or service in the world combined with aggressive prices, if nobody knows about it, you will soon fail.

The second part to making the TriFecta Exponential Growth Model work for you is to make constant forward progress. Take action to improve one of the Nine Growth Keys, then move on to the next growth key. This is a continuous improvement program, and your business will never stop growing.

To review, when do you stop marketing and improving the Nine Growth Keys? The answer is never! You can't just stop marketing once you think you have enough customers. People move, their tastes change, new competitors and new products and services enter the market, and many other factors can impact your marketplace. Maintaining a solid customer base and consistent growth requires you to make constant forward progress.

Epilogue:

Go Forth and Grow!

There you have it! The exact model and tools you need to take your business to an entirely different level in sales, profits and market share.

To excel as a business builder, you must become a life-long student of sales and marketing. What makes the TriFecta Exponential Growth Model so powerful is that it evolves as you evolve. As a "newbie" or seasoned marketing pro, applying your skills toward improving the Nine Growth Keys keeps you on track to achieving your business growth goals.

I hope this book has helped you get started with creating your own comprehensive marketing plan. Now that you have a model for success, start taking action... your business will likely benefit many thousand times more than the price you paid for this book. And you could do so much more than that.

When put into action, the TriFecta Exponential Growth Model and marketing tools covered in this book have the potential of to turn your business into a dominant force in your market. These principles and ideas will work for you just like they have worked for thousands of other businesses in hundreds of different industries and professions. But they don't work by themselves... they only work if you take action.

I have seen businesses that were struggling to make ends meet apply these marketing strategies and, in a very short time, turn their business completely around. Because the TriFecta Exponential Growth Model is based on proven business development principles and smart marketing practices, it will work for you, too.

If you rely on a sales team to generate customers, then this book will be a great tool to make your team more efficient and effective. I've used this system to help an established company in a commoditized industry increase their entire team's average conversion rate by 400%. On top of that, I had a start-up client that I assisted in product development, strategy and messaging, who immediately began closing 80% of their sales.

Understand that you are on a constant quest to add new and profitable marketing tools to your marketing program. The more tools you have working to build your business, the more successful it will become.

WILL YOU DO ME A FAVOR?

Thanks for reading this book. If you like what you've read, or even if you didn't, I want to hear from you.

As an entrepreneur myself, I want to know what you think about my products and services. All you need to do is contact my office by telephone at (225) 308-4566, or by email at "info@TriFectaMarketing.com", and tell us what you think. If you leave your email address, I will even send you a bonus gift to show my appreciation.

Russ Holder

Special Bonus #1:

FREE Gifts for You!

As an expression of gratitude for purchasing my book, I would like to offer you several special free gifts that will take *Maximizing Business Growth* to a higher level for you.

First, there are several special reports I created to augment the benefits you receive from the TriFecta Exponential Growth Model and *Maximizing Business Growth*. These special reports are:

1. *Secrets of Maximizing Growth During an Economic Meltdown: How to Gain an Incredible Competitive Advantage and Capture Market Share When All of Your Competitors are Struggling to Survive.*
2. *How to Make the Internet Work for Your Business: What Really Works on the Internet to Drive Sales and Grow Your Business.*
3. *How to Make Your Business 'Investor Ready' so You Can Cash Out Under Your Own Terms and for Maximum Profit.*
4. *20 Marketing Mistakes That are Killing Your Business: The Most Common and Likely Mistakes You are Making That are Robbing You of Profits and Growth.*
5. *The Rules of Effective* Advertising – article reprint from Russ Holder that appeared in the winter 1998 edition of *"The Marketing Advantage."*

In addition you'll receive my audio program:

6. *Secrets of Producing Exponential Growth in Your Business... Even During a Slow Economy.*

And two more "classic" books in e-book format:

7. *Scientific Advertising* by Claude Hopkins.
8. *Think and Grow Rich* by Napoleon Hill.

There are two ways to receive these eight free gifts. First, you can navigate your web browser to the following web address: **www.MaximizingBusinessGrowth.com/free-gifts.html**. Or, you can fill out the form below and fax it to (225) 308-4566. Providing this information constitutes your permission for Russ Holder and TriFecta Marketing, LLC to contact you regarding related information via the contact information you provide.

Name: _____

Business Name: _____

Address: _____

City, State, ZIP: _____

Email: _____

Phone: _____

Fax: _____

Date: _____

Special Bonus # 2:

FREE 30 Minute Growth Audit
and Opportunity Analysis

After reading *Maximizing Business Growth* you may decide that you want to take action and create your own marketing machine based on the TriFecta Exponential Growth Model. If so, you may not have to do it alone.

You may qualify to work with TriFecta Marketing to create and implement the systems, strategies and tactics contained in this book, and we give you a simple, risk free way to find out.

Maximizing Business Growth readers can request a free 30 minute coaching session to evaluate your current marketing and get some quick tips aimed at getting you on the road to the business success you want.

There are two ways to get started. Just fill out the form on the previous page and fax it to (225) 308-4566. If you write on the fax "Free Session", someone from our office will call you with scheduling options.

Your other option is to send us an email at info@TriFectaMarketing.com with the words "Free Session" in the subject line. Be sure to include your contact information so we can schedule your free coaching session.

OTHER INFORMATION FROM THE AUTHOR

For speaking engagements or consulting services, please visit www.TriFectaMarketing.com. For direct contact to Russ Holder's office, call (225) 308-4566.

Other Books by Russ Holder:
- *20 Reasons Why Your B2B Sales Stink*
- *Growing to Extremes*

Audio Programs by Russ Holder:
- *Growing to Extremes*
- *Growing Your Business During an Economic Meltdown*
- *The Easiest Way to Double Your Sales*

White Papers and Special Reports by Russ Holder:
- *20 Marketing Mistakes Killing Your Business*
- *How to Make the Internet Work for Your Business*
- *How to Double Your Advertising Results*
- *The Most Effective and Neglected Marketing Strategy*
- *The Rules of Effective Advertising*

Websites:
- www.TriFectaMarketing.com
- www.RussHolder.com

Made in the USA
Charleston, SC
06 August 2013